...AS

ADVISORY EDITOR: BETTY RADIC

PLATO (*c.* 427–347 BC) stands with Socrates and Ari
shapers of the whole intellectual tradition of the Wes
family that had long played a prominent part in Athe
would have been natural for him to follow the same c
to do so, however, disgusted by the violence and corr
political life, and sickened especially by the execution
and teacher, Socrates. Inspired by Socrates' inquiries
ethical standards, Plato sought a cure for the ills of so
but in philosophy, and arrived at his fundamental and
that those ills would never cease until philosophers
rulers philosophers. At an uncertain date in the early
he founded in Athens the Academy, the first permar
voted to philosophical research and teaching, and th
western universities. He travelled extensively, notably to Sicily as political adviser to Dionysius II, ruler of Syracuse.

Plato wrote over twenty philosophical dialogues, and there are also
extant under his name thirteen letters, whose genuineness is keenly
disputed. His literary activity extended over perhaps half a century: few
other writers have exploited so effectively the grace and precision, the
flexibility and power, of Greek prose.

SIR DESMOND LEE was born in 1908 and was a scholar at both Repton
School and at Corpus Christi College, Cambridge, where he gained a
'double first' in classics. He was a fellow and tutor at Corpus Christi and
a university lecturer there from 1937 to 1948. His lifelong association
with the college continued after he became headmaster of Clifton College
in 1948, when he was also made a life Fellow of Corpus Christi. In 1954
he left Clifton College to take up the position of headmaster at Win-
chester College where he remained until 1968. In 1959, 1960 and again in
1967 he was chairman of the Headmasters' Conference. Returning to
Cambridge in 1968 he became Senior Research Fellow at University
(now Wolfson) College, and then from 1973 until 1978 President of
Hughes Hall, Cambridge. Desmond Lee died in December 1993.

He also translated Plato's *The Republic* for Penguin Classics.

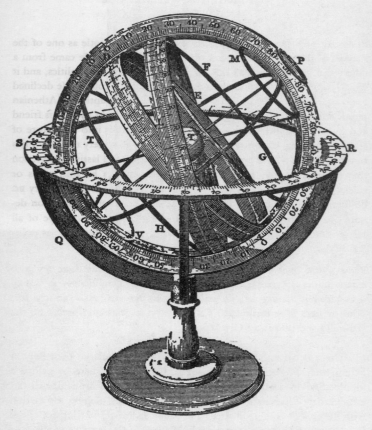

An armillary sphere (The Mansell Collection)

PLATO

TIMAEUS

AND

CRITIAS

Translated
with an introduction
and an appendix
on *Atlantis* by
DESMOND LEE

PENGUIN BOOKS

PENGUIN BOOKS

Published by the Penguin Group
Penguin Books Ltd, 27 Wrights Lane, London W8 5TZ, England
Penguin Books USA Inc., 375 Hudson Street, New York, New York 10014, USA
Penguin Books Australia Ltd, Ringwood, Victoria, Australia
Penguin Books Canada Ltd, 10 Alcorn Avenue, Toronto, Ontario, Canada M4V 3B2
Penguin Books (NZ) Ltd, 182–190 Wairau Road, Auckland 10, New Zealand

Penguin Books Ltd, Registered Offices: Harmondsworth, Middlesex, England

This translation of *Timaeus* first published 1965
Reissued with the addition of *Critias* and the Appendix on Atlantis 1971
Reprinted with revisions 1977
13 15 17 19 20 18 16 14

Copyright © H. D. P. Lee, 1965, 1971, 1977
All rights reserved

Printed in England by Clays Ltd, St Ives plc
Set in Monotype Garamond

CONTENTS

FIGURES

I am grateful to Professor Keith Guthrie, who read the introduction and the translation of the *Timaeus*, and to Mr David Steele, who read the introduction, both of whom made many helpful suggestions.

INTRODUCTION

The Timaeus:
Scope and Importance

THE *Timaeus* is a document of great importance in the history of European thought. Earlier Greek speculation about the origin of the world had, if mythical, been largely in terms of sexual reproduction or growth, or, if philosophical, been evolutionary in the sense that it accounted for the world in terms of undesigned development from material origins. In the *Timaeus* the world is created by a divinity, variously described as father, maker or craftsman. The account of his activities does not cover every department of nature; its main concern is with certain philosophical principles, with the elements of astronomy, with the structure of matter, and with human psychology and physiology. But as the first Greek account of a divine creation, containing a rational explanation of many natural processes, it remained influential throughout the period of the Ancient World, not least towards its end when it influenced the Neoplatonists and when its creator-god was easily assimilated by Christian thought to the God of Genesis. The first fifty-three chapters in a Latin translation by Chalcidius were one of the few works of classical antiquity to survive into the Dark and early Middle Ages, and in that sense its influence on European thought can be said to be continuous from its publication until the present day.

Theology

The primary purpose of the *Timaeus* is theological, that is to say, to give a religious and teleological account of the origin of the world and of the phenomena of nature. In the *Laws* Plato sharply criticizes those who account for the natural world and its processes in purely material terms, attributing them to necessity or chance, both of which share the common characteristic of ex-

7

cluding intelligence or design; the Creator in the *Timaeus* is in himself an assertion of the opposite view, that the power behind the universe is that of a divine purpose. But the Creator is in many ways a shadowy figure. Under the different titles of God, father, maker or craftsman he represents a concept of *creation* new in Greece. Earlier cosmogonists had, as we have seen, used metaphors from human or animal reproduction; gods and goddesses begat and produced children, earth gave birth to 'high mountains and unharvested sea',[1] the Orphic world-egg was laid and hatched. And following the mythologers the natural philosophers had supposed that the material substance of nature, whatever it might be, grew, by some inherent but often ill-defined power, into the world we know. The analogy in the *Timaeus* is no longer that of a reproduction or growth, but of the deliberate constructive activity of a craftsman. The creator-god, like the craftsman, needs material to work on – the antecedent chaos, the 'nurse of becoming'; he needs a plan according to which to work – the model, 'the eternal living creature'; he is not omnipotent, for his material limits his operations – reason has to 'persuade' necessity: but within those limitations he produces the best he can. That is the underlying picture, and we are perhaps unwise to demythologize it too far. We may notice that the creator-god is never spoken of as an object of worship, that he is never equated with the supreme God of the Greek pantheon, Zeus, that he is not the omnipotent God of Jewish and Christian tradition. But we are unwise if we try to equate him with Reason in the world soul, or to argue (as many have done, since the time of Plato's immediate successors) that he is only a symbol and that Plato did not intend the idea of creation to be taken seriously. His language (p. 42) does not suggest this, and we do best to recognize that much of the *Timaeus* is myth and to be cautious in interpreting it in non-mythological terms.

The Greek pre-conception, from which Plato would start, was that of a supreme God, Zeus, whose powers were not unlimited in spite of his supremacy. Beneath him were a number of major Gods – the Greek pantheon usually included twelve – and beneath them again minor Gods, daemons, spirits and (since the line between divine and human might sometimes be crossed) heroes. Plato's creator-god is never called Zeus; but it is the

1. Hesiod, *Theogony*, 129.

natural and easy assumption that he is the supreme divinity in the world he creates. He is not alone, for he himself creates not only the traditional Gods, subordinate to himself, but other divine beings also – the world soul, the souls of the stars, and (again bridging human and divine) the immortal element in the human soul. The world of the *Timaeus* is one in which there is a hierarchy of divine beings, and as such it fitted in with the accepted Greek pattern and itself in turn influenced later speculations. Astrology, which regarded the stars and heavenly bodies as divine, could find the same belief in the *Timaeus* – a belief, incidentally, which makes its first major appearance in Greece in Plato; in traditional Greek religion the heavenly bodies as such play little part. Neoplatonism with its elaborate spiritual hierarchy could again look to the *Timaeus*, and so too, in a different way, could the elaborate hierarchies of Christian theology.

Two other points should be mentioned under this heading. (1) The soul, as divine, is immortal, but destined not for a single life on earth but for many. The details of Plato's views on transmigration must be looked for elsewhere, for example the myth of Er in the *Republic*. But the doctrine is still part of the theological structure of the *Timaeus*.

(2) There is a close correspondence between macrocosm and microcosm, that is, between the structure and behaviour of the world as a whole and that of the human-creature in particular. This shows itself especially in the circles of Same and Different, which exist both in the world soul and in the human soul, in the sphere of the universe and the sphere of the head. But the general doctrine of the correspondence of macrocosm and microcosm runs right through the dialogue and was one that was to have a long and often unhappy influence.

Philosophy

One of the basic premises of Plato's philosophy is the distinction between two orders of reality, Being and Becoming; and from that premise the *Timaeus* starts (p. 40). Ever since Homer compared the generations of men to falling leaves the Greeks had been sharply and intensely aware of the transitoriness of human life, and this awareness partly colours Plato's dismissal of the world of ordinary perception as not fully real. But the distinction also has its base in philosophy, in the contrast between the truths of logic and of mathematics on the one hand and those of empirical knowledge on the other; it is to this contrast that Plato appeals on the only occasion in the *Timaeus* when any proof of the distinction is offered (p. 71). The real world, the world of Being, contains the Platonic Forms, the objects of rational understanding and of the operations of mathematics and logic with which Plato had become increasingly preoccupied as he grew older. The world of Becoming contains all the things perceived by our senses, about which no certain and final knowledge is possible.

The relation between the two worlds remains one of the problems of Plato's philosophy until the end. In the *Timaeus* it is coloured by the creator simile. Just as a craftsman must have a plan or model to work to, so the divine creator models the world of Becoming, which he creates, on the world of Being. The model to which he works is described (p. 54) as an 'intelligible living creature'; by which Plato must mean a complex system of Forms, containing within itself all the subordinate Forms whose likeness we can trace in the world of Becoming. The conception is not an easy one and it is not easy to see what is the place of the 'intelligible living creature' in the world of Forms as a whole; its *function* is to act as model for the creator, and its presence in the *Timaeus* is perhaps due as much to the requirements of the craftsman analogy as to any philosophic principle.

Having dealt with the craftsman's model Plato goes on to his material, which is initially (pp. 43–4) described as the four elements, earth, air, fire, and water. This simple description is qualified later in the passage describing the Receptacle of Becoming, when we learn that it consists of an indeterminate substance in confused motion, which only takes the determinate form of the four elements when reduced to the four geometrical figures by the Creator. Indeed to call it substance is an over-statement and it is subsequently described as space (p. 71), though as space in which disorderly motion is taking place (p. 72). It is also closely associated with necessity or the indeterminate cause.

The meaning of all this in more philosophical terms is not easy to define precisely, just because there is so large an element of myth in it. We have seen that to demythologize the *Timaeus* in a way that would ignore the creation story is to go too far; Plato can most safely be supposed to mean what he said when he speaks of the universe having a beginning. But to say what that means is not easy. Plato was aware of the close connection between time and time measurement. Can we speak of one without the other? And if not, are we not bound to say that 'time came into being with the heavens' (p. 52), that is, that time in the sense we use it cannot be conceived without the instruments, processes, and movements by which we measure it? Aristotle, with his sharper distinction between time and motion, took the argument a stage further; but it is not yet concluded.[1] But we can correlate certain aspects of Plato's creation myth with certain features of the world as we know it. The function of the creator is to account for the *intelligibility* of the universe. Plato thought that the universe was an intelligible system – we can, after all, *understand* it; and that this can only be accounted for by there being an intelligent force underlying it. And for him intelligence carried the two further implications of purposive design and goodness. So the creator's motive for creation is to make things as good as possible (p. 42), and where we can trace divine goodness we can trace divine purpose (p. 96).

The other factor in creation, the material, 'necessity', 'the indeterminate cause', must be understood against this background. The material which the craftsman uses will have certain properties of its own, irrelevant to his purpose, which may produce side-effects. The steel, which must have certain properties if it is to make a satisfactory tool, will rust. This is not part of the purpose of its manufacture; it is a side-effect, inevitable but irrelevant. A similar idea reappears in Aristotle's 'hypothetical necessity'. Material of a certain kind is *necessary if* certain purposes are to be achieved; qualities it may have outside what those purposes require are irrelevant and unpredictable in terms of those purposes.

So far we are still in the realm of metaphor and it is not easy to give metaphor a philosophic meaning. Taylor and Cornford[2] take rather different views, but agree in regarding 'necessity' as an *arbitrary* factor in the universe, something for which we can find no explanation. Both agree again in regarding this factor as irreducible in the sense that it will never disappear; there will always be *something* we cannot explain. Cornford[3] describes neces-

1. Cf. G. T. Whitrow, *Natural History of Time*, Ch. I.

2. Taylor, *A Commentary on Plato's Timaeus*, pp. 300–301, Cornford, *Plato's Cosmology*, p. 160 ff.

3. p. 172.

sity as 'the indeterminate, the inconstant, the anomalous, that which can neither be understood nor predicted'. And when Plato describes physical science as a 'likely story' (p. 42) he may be doing no more than calling attention to this factor in the physical world and our knowledge of it. But we can perhaps explain his meaning a little more fully. He attached great importance (as we have seen) to the difference between mathematical and logical knowledge on the one hand and empirical knowledge on the other, and regarded empirical knowledge as unsatisfactory because it had not the self-validating and demonstrable character of mathematics and logic. And when he calls physical science a 'likely story' he is to some extent implying that it is unsatisfactory because it lacks this character. In so far as he is doing that he is mistaken, though his mistake is one that has, in different ways, been constantly repeated; for philosophers have been too prone to require *all* knowledge to conform to a *single* set of criteria. On the other hand, in so far as he means that it is in the nature of scientific hypotheses that they should be in a certain sense provisional, he is saying something perfectly true and acceptable to the scientist.

This is perhaps as much as can be safely said. What is interesting, in conclusion, to note is that it is to the element of uncertainty in empirical knowledge that he gives the name 'necessity'; those unvarying regularities in nature which we are inclined to attribute to what we call 'mechanical necessity' are to him the proof of rational and purposive design.

Astronomy

The most obvious and impressive of these regularities is the movement of the heavenly bodies, and it is therefore not surprising that they should be attributed to the action of a divine intelligent world soul. But a further reason for the attribution is to be found in Plato's dynamics. To the Greek the most obvious thing about motion was that it needed a force to cause it. He lived in a world where there were no machines, in which there was little wheeled transport, and in which such concepts as velocity, mass, or acceleration were not and could hardly be understood. It is not surprising that when Aristotle came to frame his theory of motion the problem should seem to him to be the overcoming of inertia, and that his typical example is that of a body of men pushing a ship down the shore to launch it; so that his theory (if one may so call it) is framed in terms of the relations between force, motion, and the resistance of the medium in which the motion takes place. It follows that for motion to be continuous a continuous force must be operating, a principle which Plato accepted as completely as Aristotle, and which profoundly affected the astronomical systems of them both. For it at once raises the question, what is the force causing the continuous and regular motions of the heavenly bodies? Plato considered that bodies in motion must either have that motion imparted to them by another body, or have within them a self-acting source of motion. Observation showed him that the only things capable of generating motion without external impulse were living things, whose differentiating characteristic was that they had ψυχή, life or soul. In this later philosophy, therefore, the soul is regarded as the only originating source of motion, the only self-mover; and soul consequently is regarded as the force which keeps the heavenly bodies in motion.

The known astronomical motions for which Plato had to account were of three kinds: first, the daily rotation of all the heavenly bodies from east to west; second, the apparent movement of sun, moon and planets from west to east against the background of the fixed stars; and third, certain individual variations (e.g. retrogradations) of particular planets. At this point logic and astronomy meet. In his later dialogues, in particular in the *Sophist*, Plato had come to the conclusion that the two basic kinds of judgement were judgements of conjunction and disjunction, their simplest forms being those in which we assert that a thing has a property (conjunction or affirmation) or that it has not (disjunction or negation). These therefore must be the two basic kinds of mental process (feelings and appetites belong to the mortal parts of the soul and may consequently be ignored) and we shall expect to find them in the world-soul as much as in any other soul. But, as we have seen, there are, if we omit individual variations, two main kinds of movement observable in the heavenly bodies. So we arrive at the circles of Same and Different in the world soul and the human soul, which are able, on a cosmic scale, to account for the two basic types of astronomical movement, and, in the human soul, for the two basic types of judgement and so for rational thought.

The details of Plato's construction are complicated, but its

main outlines are simple. When the soul-stuff has been manufactured, it is cut into two strips, rather as one might cut a length
of dress material. The strips are bent round to form rings and
the two rings set one within the other at an angle, to represent
the difference in angle between the axes of the ecliptic and of the
fixed stars. The inner ring is then cut into seven further strips, to
represent sun, moon, and planets. Both rings are in constant
motion (being soul) but in opposite directions; and the subdivisions of the second ring (the Different) move at different
though constant speeds (to correspond with the observed
differences in speed in the motion of the planets from west to
east).

This idea of the planets moving on rings was not a new one.
Anaximander had supposed the sun and moon to be carried on
rings like the felloe of a wheel, and there are traces of a similar
doctrine elsewhere. The idea of a ring does not suit the fixed stars
as well as it suits the planets, and it is doubtful whether Plato
meant it to be taken literally. From earliest times the heavens had
been regarded as a dome, and it was not a long step from that,
once the idea of a central, freely suspended earth was put forward,
to suppose them to be a sphere made of some translucent material
– at this period fire or air, later crystal. Plato is emphatic in his
assertion that the shape of the universe is spherical, and we do
best to imagine his astronomical system as one in which there is
a central earth, with a sphere carrying the fixed stars as its outer
limit, and with the planets carried round on rings within the
sphere. The nearest representation of what he had in mind is
given by an armillary sphere (cf. frontispiece), though this was
devised for other purposes and does not show the planetary
rings separately.

The heavenly bodies all share the movement of the Same, the
daily rotation from east to west; the planetary rings are carried
round by the movement of the outer sphere of the stars. But sun,
moon and planets also have their westward rotations, at different
speeds. These are due, as a whole, to the movement of the Different; but their varying speeds and the irregularities of their
motion (including retrogradation) are due to their being divine
beings composed of soul and body, whose souls exercise their
power of movement independently of the Different.[1] The ob-

1. See note on p. 52.

served track of a planet is thus the result of a combination of three separate motions.

This analysis of a single *observed* movement into a combination of two or more actual movements had been one of the triumphs of the Pythagoreans. It was taken up by Plato and carried still further by Eudoxus, who as a member of the Academy took up Plato's challenge to produce an analysis which would 'save the phenomena', that is, account in terms of a combination of movements for the observed facts. This he did with his system of concentric spheres, which was adopted by Aristotle and dominated astronomy till the time of Copernicus. It is perhaps strange that it should make no appearance in Plato's works; but Eudoxus did not die until after Plato, who may have been slow to adopt the theory of a junior contemporary, which may not yet have been produced at the time when the *Timaeus* was written. What is more important than this historical detail of the relations between Plato and Eudoxus is that it was at this time in the Academy that European mathematical astronomy was born; for the line of descent leads directly from Eudoxus to the great Hellenistic astronomers and so to Ptolemy. The system of the *Timaeus* is now a historical curiosity: but it marks a decisive step in the development of scientific astronomy.

Structure of Matter

The theory that the four elements, earth, air, fire and water, are the material constituents of the world had been put forward already, before Plato's day, by Empedocles. Others had suggested a single constituent, water or air; but by Plato's day it was accepted that the ultimate constituents must be several in number, and in the absence of the techniques of chemical analysis the four elements were a fairly obvious choice, a choice to be endorsed by Aristotle. About this part of Plato's view of matter there is little originality; nor was he original in suggesting a form of the atomic theory, which Leucippus and Democritus had already put forward before him, though, unlike them, he limited the number of forms which the basic particles could take to four of the five regular solids. This limitation and the association of different elements with different types of atom is important. The association was not made again till Dalton, and then it formed the basis of modern chemistry. The main interest of

Plato's scheme, however, lies in its attempt, crude though it is, to apply mathematics to nature. The relation between his geometrical shapes and their material is not clear; how can solids be made up of and disintegrate into triangles? He has not sufficiently distinguished between geometrical figure and material particle. But the scheme is an ingenious attempt to account for differences between and transformations of different types of matter in mathematical terms, and the process of thought is one that is still useful. Mendeleev's periodic table of the elements was a scheme in which the physical and chemical properties of the elements were found to fall into a mathematical pattern; and sub-nuclear particles have recently been plotted, according to two of their important properties, to conform to simple geometrical patterns.[1]

For the details of Plato's scheme the reader may be referred to the translation and to the figures illustrating it (p. 73ff.). Though details are largely a matter of historic interest, there was an insight here which could not come to fruition until the techniques of experimental measurement gave the mathematician reliable evidence to work upon.

Psychology and Physiology

Plato first speaks of three parts of the soul or mind in the *Republic*. There the division is not very precisely made and he seems to be thinking rather of three elements in mental conflict than of three exactly defined parts; there are large areas of human experience, e.g. sensation and perception, which he does not attempt to touch. The comparison of the soul to a chariot with a driver and two horses in the *Phaedrus* perhaps indicates a sharper division into parts, and in the *Timaeus* the three parts are not only distinguished but located in different parts of the body. The powers of reason and decision (for Plato these always went together; he has no conception of the will as a separate function) are situated in the head. They constitute the divine and immortal part of the soul, which, like the world-soul, has its circles of Same and Different, enabling it to make the basic

1. P. T. Matthews in *New Scientist*, 20 February 1964. That one ten-member set of particles should fall into a triangular pattern arranged as the Pythagoreans arranged the decad is a coincidence that would have delighted Plato.

types of judgement, affirmation and negation, and so to proceed
to the whole business of rational thought; but because of its
connection with a mortal body the immortal part and its circles
are liable to disturbance and consequent error. Little is said about
transmigration, though it is still an essential part of Plato's
belief. Human souls at their first creation are told (p. 58) that
any failure in their first incarnation as man will lead to re-
incarnation as women or lower animals, who are created for the
purpose at the end of the story.

The two other parts of the soul are located in the heart and
belly, and are specifically said to be mortal. They comprise very
roughly (and Plato in the *Timaeus* is more concerned with phys-
iological location than psychological detail) the emotions and
feelings on the one hand and the physical appetites on the other;
and being mortal they are closely connected with the physio-
logical processes of the parts in which they are situated. Plato
also has a good deal to say about sensation (pp. 87–95), but he
knew nothing of the nervous system and his views bear little
relation to fact, though by making the head the seat of intelligence and so (by implication) of the nervous system he
guessed better than Aristotle did after him. Perhaps the two
most interesting points are the insistence on the close connection
between body and mind and so between mental and physical
disease, and the use of this connection to give a new interpretation to the old Socratic paradox 'no man does wrong willingly',
to the effect that wrongdoing is often not due to deliberate
choice but to a failure to train and coordinate mind and body in
their mutual relation (p. 117f.).

Throughout his account of sensation and the involved description of respiration and digestion contained in the fish-trap simile
it is important to remember how limited in Plato's day was knowledge of the details of human anatomy. There was little dissection
of the human body in the ancient world. In Hellenistic times it
was practised to some extent by Herophilus and Erisistratus; but
Galen drew most of his knowledge from the dissection of
monkeys, from which his views of the human body were in-
ferred. It is not surprising therefore that much of the latter part
of the *Timaeus* seems to the modern reader so wide of the mark
as to be of little interest even to historical curiosity.

Ancient and Modern

What is of more interest than the question *how* Plato was wrong, is the rather different question *why* he was wrong. To answer it in full would involve a detailed study of the limitations of Greek science and of the question why, after starting on the road of rational inquiry into the natural world, it seems to falter and run off into unprofitable by-ways. The most that can be done here is to list a few very general considerations.

'Rational' and 'scientific' are distinct. For though to be scientific one must be rational, to be rational is not, in itself, to be scientific. The scientific method evolved step by step in the later Middle Ages and during and after the Renaissance. Its essential component is, as Bacon pointed out, that of experiment. And the full implications of the experimental method are complicated, involving the deliberate observation of processes in artificial isolation, eventually in the artificial isolation of the laboratory; scientific knowledge is very largely laboratory-based knowledge. The laboratory in turn presupposes a far higher level of technology than any reached in the ancient world; it is impossible without some degree of the industrialization which it will itself accelerate and promote.

The limitation placed on the development of Greek science by the level of technology in the ancient world has been underestimated and its causes misunderstood. It is commonly said that the Greeks had an aristocratic contempt for manual labour and that this discouraged them from experiment and hindered the development of technology. But the controlling classes in seventeenth-century England, when modern technological development started, were not particularly inclined to manual labour; and if the classes actually engaged in the use of technological processes in the ancient world had any inhibitions, these were certainly not aristocratic. The Roman contractor was a fairly rough type, often a freedman; and he would have welcomed technological innovation if it would have helped him (as it would) in the job he was doing, and enabled him to make more money. The reason why technical processes did not develop further in the ancient world is to be found in the history of technology itself rather than in external psychological or social causes.[1]

1. E.g. the existence of slavery; for, as Sambursky (*Physical World of*

Perhaps the main single cause was the weakness of ancient metallurgy. The discovery of cast-iron in the fourteenth century was as great a break with the past as was the previous discovery of how to smelt iron in usable quantities and the later discovery how to smelt it with coke. The ancient world suffered from all the limitations of the first phase of the Iron Age. And if the devices described, for example, in Hero's *Mechanics*, strike us as toys rather than means for exploiting nature, it was in part because there was no suitable metal available for their construction on a larger scale. But there were other limitations besides those of metallurgical technique. There were few instruments of precision, no accurate clocks, no glass suitable for chemical experiment (until a comparatively late date): there was no mariner's compass, no gunpowder, no printing. Even the horse, as a source of power, was of limited usefulness because of the inefficiency of ancient harness. The list could be prolonged, and no particular item in it is decisive in itself; but between them they add up to a formidable barrier to the development of experimental science, which needs the more sophisticated technological basis which between them they afford. That basis was gradually developed during the later Middle Ages and by the Renaissance a further advance was possible.

But a higher level of technology was not all that was required. It no doubt made it possible, or easier, for Galileo to come by the equipment he used for his investigations – the telescope, the iron balls to roll down inclined planes. But an alteration of viewpoint was also necessary. Sambursky[1] has remarked that while the Greeks tied science to philosophy, Galileo and the seventeenth century again untied them. Science had to spend a time under the tutelage of philosophy to gain its freedom from the control of myth and religion. But philosophy is concerned to understand rather than to change; and the Greek, for this, and

---

the Greeks, p. 226) points out, the Egyptians did achieve considerable advances in technology and yet were a slave-owning society. An excellent discussion of the topics dealt with in this section will be found in his chapter on the Limits of Greek Science. See also my articles on 'Science, philosophy and technology in the Greco-Roman World', *Greece and Rome*, April–October 1973.

1. op. cit., p. 224.

perhaps for other temperamental reasons, was content to understand nature if he could, but had no wish either to change or control her. The experimental method therefore eluded him. For the experimental method, as we have seen, requires active interference – the study of processes in artificial isolation, in the unnatural environment of the laboratory, which requires increasingly elaborate man-made apparatus. This artificiality is something quite foreign to the temperament of the Greek. He was prepared to observe but not to interfere. So the science in which he made the greatest advance was astronomy, where interference is neither necessary nor possible, and what is required is repeated observation and mathematical analysis. Simply because he was content to observe in the hope of understanding he never hit on the method which true understanding requires.

In this lies the main difference between the ancient and the modern approach. But there are two other points worth noting. Great as was the Greeks' achievement in mathematics in many respects, and skilful as was their use of it in descriptive astronomy, their numerical notation remained clumsy and so their attempts to describe nature mathematically were limited and ineffective. They could not have developed the mechanics of the seventeenth century because they had not the mathematical apparatus to do it. But in any case their interest in mechanics was limited; for ancient science (and this is the second point) suffered from what may be called a biological preoccupation. We tend to forget how much of the *Timaeus* is devoted to physiology and psychology; and while it was being written Aristotle had already embarked on the study of biology which was his greatest scientific achievement and which gave a particular twist to his whole philosophy. We have already noted in the *Timaeus* the doctrine of the correspondence between macrocosm and microcosm. This inevitably meant that the physical world was interpreted in anthropocentric terms, in terms of purpose and function that may have a place in biology and psychology, but are not similarly applicable in the physical sciences. The freeing of the physical sciences from these and other conceptions inappropriate to them was essential before modern science could begin. Of the Greek viewpoint the *Timaeus* was typical, just as it was also influential in forming it.

INTRODUCTION

Later Influence

The limitations within which ancient science worked were only overcome in a gradual process culminating in the nineteenth century; and until they were overcome the *Timaeus* stood as an example of what could be achieved within them, and also, in some respects – as for example in its insistence on the importance of mathematics for the understanding of nature – as a pointer to the way in which they were to be overcome. It retained its direct influence on the ancient world so long as Greek was understood and read and when East and West separated and the West lost the knowledge of Greek, survived into the Dark and Middle Ages in Chalcidius' Latin version and a fragment translated by Cicero. The story of its influence thereafter until the Renaissance is briefly told in the following paragraphs:

This dialogue, or rather its first part, was studied and quoted throughout the Middle Ages, and there was hardly a medieval library of any standing which had not a copy of Chalcidius' version and sometimes also a copy of the fragment translated by Cicero. Although these facts are well known, their significance for the history of ideas has perhaps not been sufficiently grasped by historians. The *Timaeus* with its attempted synthesis of the religious teleological justification of the world and the rational exposition of creation was, throughout the earlier Middle Ages, the starting point and guide for the first groping efforts towards a scientific cosmology. Around this dialogue and the exposition of Chalcidius accompanying it in many manuscripts, there grew up an extensive literature of commentaries. . .

The desire for a more rational explanation of the universe found its expression in the attempts to harmonize the Platonic and Mosaic narratives and to interpret the biblical account in Genesis by means of the Greek scientific categories and concepts which had become part of Western thought, mainly by way of the Latin *Timaeus* and its commentator. These tendencies culminated in the twelfth century in the School of Chartres which exercised a profound influence on teachers of the arts in Paris in the following century. The *Timaeus* was read in this faculty with explanations from William of Conches's commentary until, in 1255 at the latest, it was superseded in the official order of studies by the Aristotelian corpus, though it is to be found occasionally in University manuscripts of later date.

The influence of the masters of Chartres, latent for two centuries, revives in the doctrines of Nicholas of Cusa, who, more perhaps than any other individual thinker, contributed to the formation of the so-called modern cosmology. This connection between the Renaissance philosopher, in the judgement of contemporaries the 'grande Platoniste', and the Platonists of the twelfth century is a striking instance of the continuity of Platonic tradition. Through Cusanus certain of their doctrines became known to Copernicus, as we are able to prove by the marginal notes in his copy of Bovillus's *Liber de intellectu*. The adherents of the 'Nova scientia', when they chose Plato as their guide in their fight against Aristotelianism, could take up the threads of a Platonic tradition which had never been entirely lost in the Latin world.

But apart from their value for the development of science, the *Timaeus* and the literature to which it gave rise preserved, through the centuries in which an attitude of contempt towards the visible world was prevalent in the accepted Church doctrine, the memory of the Hellenic appreciation of the rational beauty of the universe. It was precisely this fusion of the rational-mathematical, the aesthetic and the religious elements in the contemplation of the universe, this glorification of the cosmos, that appealed to the philosophers of the Renaissance and deeply influenced their cosmological outlook.[1]

The Timaeus *and the* Critias*: Relationship, Date and Form*

The *Timaeus* has long been regarded as one of the last works which Plato wrote. On evidence of style, it and its continuation the *Critias* have commonly been grouped with the *Laws* (his last work); and though this grouping has been doubted, the case against it has not been established. It seems certain therefore that the *Timaeus* belongs to the last main group of works which Plato wrote, and so that it was written in the last ten or dozen years of his life; and likely that it and the *Critias* were the last works he wrote before he embarked on the *Laws*, which he left unfinished on his death in 348 B.C. In form it is a dialogue with four speakers, Socrates, Timaeus himself, Critias, and Hermocrates. But after an introductory section the dialogue form is dropped and the main body of the work is a continuous exposition by Timaeus. A sequel is promised, the *Critias*, which remained unfinished; and in the *Critias* a third work, in which

1. R. Klibansky, *Continuity of the Platonic Tradition*, pp. 28–9. See also C. S. Lewis, *The Discarded Image*.

Hermocrates was to be the main speaker, is forecast. The *Timaeus* opens with an introductory dialogue in which Socrates recalls in outline a conversation of the day before in which he had discussed the institutions of an ideal state. The outline covers fairly completely the social and political provisions made in the *Republic*, but omits its psychology, metaphysics, and much else. The festival which is the dramatic date of the *Republic* is separated by two months from either of the two possible festivals which are the dramatic date of the *Timaeus*, and there is no reason to link the two dialogues closely together.

Socrates is anxious to see his ideal society in action, and in reply Critias gives an outline of the Atlantis myth, and suggests that Socrates' ideal society may be found in the Athens of the myth. He proposes, therefore, that by way of prelude Timaeus, who is expert in these matters, shall 'tell the story of the universe till the creation of man', thus giving the theological and metaphysical background against which human society must operate; he himself will follow with a fuller exposition of the Atlantis myth, and will in turn be followed, as the introductory pages of the *Critias* show, by Hermocrates. We have no definite indication what the subject of Hermocrates' contribution was to be. The most plausible conjecture is Cornford's. The Atlantis myth ends with the destruction of mankind, except for a few survivors in the mountains; 'taking up the story at this point what could Hermocrates do, if not describe the re-emergence of culture in the Greece of prehistoric and historic times?'[1] But this is very much the theme of the third and subsequent books of the *Laws*. And so Cornford suggests that Plato, finding that the material for the third dialogue of the trilogy was outgrowing its formal limits, abandoned the task of completing it (the *Critias* as we have it stops in mid-sentence) and turned to his last major work, the *Laws*. The Academy had started as a school for statesmen[2] and man in society remained at the centre of Plato's thoughts till he died. The place of the story of Atlantis in this general pattern is discussed more fully in the Appendix, p. 146.

1. *Plato's Cosmology*, p. 7.
2. See the Introduction to my translation of the *Republic* (Penguin Books), pp. 17 ff.

Style

The two dialogues have particular difficulties for the translator. The Greek is by common consent difficult. In the *Timaeus* in particular Plato is dealing with an unfamiliar subject – nowhere else does he deal at length with the origin or nature of the physical world; he is telling a creation story, which leads in places to the use of more elevated language than a more ordinary theme. And these factors may account for some of the peculiar difficulties of the language which he uses. But Plato's style also changed as he grew older. The changes include not only unconscious tricks of usage, which because they are unconscious are invaluable to stylometry in its attempt to order the dialogues chronologically; they also include a number of conscious devices, like avoidance of hiatus and deliberate adjustment of word order, which make for less easy reading. Add to this a certain stiffness, a lack of the ease and vitality that characterized the earlier dialogues, and you have in brief the main characteristics of the original Greek: elaborate, often deliberately contrived, dealing with unfamiliar material for which no ready vocabulary existed, sometimes solemn, and lacking in the lively clarity and natural vigour of earlier work.

Faced with these difficulties the translator's first duty is to make out the meaning as clearly as he can with the aid of the commentators. He must then decide how far he should try to reproduce the characteristics of the original in his English version. Of the two most recent translators, Taylor tries to catch the solemnity of the original by a certain archaism. But Plato did not seem archaic when he wrote, and archaism conveys a wrong atmosphere and does not make for clear understanding.[1] Cornford is direct and full, concerned that the reader shall have in English all the detail of what Plato said;[2] and there is his commentary to explain, add, or subtract. For a reader without a commentary, what Plato meant is as important as what he said, and the full detail of a literal rendering can not only seem unnatural in English but also make understanding more difficult.

1. Besides tending to absurdity: cf. the phrase 'have no joyaunce of each other'. Taylor, *Timaeus and Critias*, p. 88.

2. 'My aim has been to render Plato's words as closely as I can', op. cit., p. vii.

No attempt has therefore been made here to reproduce the peculiar character of the Greek; the object has been to discover Plato's meaning and express it in the sort of English we actually use. Something is thereby lost, and at times the complications of the Greek may distort the English. But it seems the best way to serve the modern reader, and even in plain language something of the grandeur of Plato's thought may be apparent.

*

The translation has been made from Burnet's text in the Oxford Classical Texts, with a note of any variations adopted. The two main modern commentaries in English on the *Timaeus* are Taylor's *A Commentary on Plato's Timaeus*, and Cornford's *Plato's Cosmology*. I have used these constantly and my debt to them will be apparent; especially my debt to Cornford, whose work is the later of the two and whose lectures on the *Timaeus* I once attended.

TIMAEUS

CHARACTERS IN THE DIALOGUE

SOCRATES.

TIMAEUS, of Locri, in southern Italy. There is no
evidence for his historical existence, but he may
have been modelled on Archytas of Tarentum,
philosopher and statesman, whom Plato met on
his first visit to Sicily (about 388 B.C.).

CRITIAS. Plato's maternal great grandfather.

HERMOCRATES. Syracusan statesman and soldier,
who took a prominent part in the defeat of the
Athenian expedition against Sicily (413–410 B.C.).

The dramatic date of the dialogue is about 425 B.C.,
when Socrates was about 45.

*It is customary to refer to Plato's works by reference to
the pages of an early edition, that of Stephanus, 1578.
These numbers are printed in the margin of this translation.*

1. *Introductory Conversation (a). Socrates has, on the previous day, described an ideal society. He feels that his description lacked reality, which he calls on the others present to provide.*

The ideal society is very like that outlined in Plato's Republic.

SOCRATES: One, two, three – but where, my dear Timaeus, is the fourth of my guests of yesterday who were to entertain me today?

TIMAEUS: He's fallen sick, Socrates; otherwise he would never willingly have missed today's discussion.

SOCRATES: Then if he's away it is up to you and the others to play his part as well as your own.

TIMAEUS: Yes; we'll certainly do our best. For it would not be fair, after the hospitality you showed your guests yesterday, if the rest of us were not ready to entertain you in return.

SOCRATES: Do you remember, then, the subject I set you and its scope?

TIMAEUS: Part of it; and you are here to remind us of anything we have forgotten. Better still, if it's not too much trouble, give us a brief summary of the discussion, to fortify our memory.

SOCRATES: I will. Yesterday my main object was to describe my view of the ideal state and its citizens.

TIMAEUS: And your description was much to our liking, Socrates.

SOCRATES: We began, did we not, by separating the farmers and the other craftsmen from the defence forces?

TIMAEUS: Yes.

SOCRATES: And we assigned to each class, as being natural to it, a single appropriate occupation or craft. So

those whose duty it was to defend the community would be its sole guardians against threats of injury, whether external or internal: they would be gentle in administering justice to
18 their subjects, who were their natural friends, and tough in fighting battles against external enemies.

TIMAEUS: Certainly.

SOCRATES: And to ensure the appropriate gentleness and toughness in their behaviour to each, we said that the character of the guardians must combine the spirited and the philosophic to a rare degree.

TIMAEUS: Yes.

SOCRATES: As for their up-bringing, they were to be trained physically and mentally in all studies suitable for the purpose.

TIMAEUS: Of course.

SOCRATES: Having been so brought up they must never, we said, regard gold or silver or anything else as their own private property, but earn as a garrison a modest wage, sufficient for their simple needs, in return for the safeguard they afforded to those under their protection. They were to share all expenditure and live a common life together, devoting their attention wholly to excellence, freed from all other preoccupations.

TIMAEUS: That was what we said.

SOCRATES: And we had something to say about the women, too. Their characters were to be moulded similarly to men's, and they were to share the same occupations both in war and in the rest of life.

TIMAEUS: We said that too.

SOCRATES: I expect you remember what was said about the production of children, because it was unusual. We laid it down that marriages and children should be shared in common by all, and arranged that no one should recognize any child born as their own, but that all should regard themselves as related to everyone else. So all those born within an appropriate period would regard each other as brothers and sisters, anyone born earlier than themselves as parents and grandparents, and anyone born later than themselves as children and grandchildren.

TIMAEUS: Yes, the provisions you describe are easy to remember.

SOCRATES: And to ensure that their natural endowment 19 should from the start be the best possible, you will remember that we said that the men and women in authority should secretly arrange the lots so that bad and good men would be allocated for mating at marriage festivals to women like themselves, and prevent any possible consequent ill-feeling by letting it be supposed that the allocation was due to chance.

TIMAEUS: I remember.

SOCRATES: You will remember too that we said that the children of the good were to be brought up and cared for, and those of the bad distributed secretly among the rest of the community; and the rulers were to keep an eye on the children as they grew up and promote in turn any who deserved it, and degrade into the places of the promoted any in their own ranks who seemed unworthy of their position.

TIMAEUS: So we said.

SOCRATES: Is that an adequate summary of yesterday's discussion, Timaeus, or is there anything that we have omitted?

TIMAEUS: There is nothing, Socrates; you have covered the ground completely.

SOCRATES: Let me now go on to tell you how I feel about the society we have described. My feelings are rather like those of a man who has seen some splendid animals, either in a picture or really alive but motionless, and wants to see them moving and engaging in some of the activities for which they appear to be formed. That's exactly what I feel about the society we have described. I would be glad to hear some account of it engaging in transactions with other states, waging war successfully and showing in the process all the qualities one would expect from its system of education and training, both in action and negotiation with its rivals.

Now, my dear Critias and Hermocrates, I know that I am myself incapable of giving any adequate account of this kind of our city and its citizens. This, as far as I am concerned, is not surprising; but in my opinion the same is true of the poets, past and present. Not that I have a low opinion of poets in general, but it is clear that in all kinds of representation one represents best and most easily what lies within one's experience, while what lies outside that experience is difficult to represent in action and even more difficult in words. The sophists, again, I have always thought to be very ready with glowing descriptions of every kind, but I am afraid that, because they have travelled so much and never had a home of their own, they may fail to grasp the true qualities which those who are philosophers and statesmen would show in action and in negotiation in the conduct of peace and war. There remain people of your kind, who are by nature and education imbued with philosophy and states-

20 manship. For Timaeus here comes from the Italian Locris, a very well run city, where he is second to none in wealth and birth: there he has enjoyed the highest office and distinction the city can offer, and has also in my opinion reached the highest eminence in philosophy. Critias, of course, all of us here know to be no amateur in these matters, while there are many witnesses to assure us that Hermocrates is well qualified in them also, both by his natural gifts and by his education. I had this in mind yesterday when I agreed so readily to your request for an account of my ideal society: I knew that there was no one more fitted to provide the sequel to it than you – you are the only living people who could adequately describe my city fighting a war worthy of her. So when I had done what was asked of me, I set you the task I have just described. You agreed to put your heads together, and return my hospitality today; and here I am dressed in my best and looking forward to what I am about to receive.

2. *Introductory Conversation (b). The Atlantis Myth; the ideal society existed once in ancient Athens. The reply to Socrates will comprise a cosmological introduction by Timaeus, followed by a fuller account of Atlantis and ancient Athens by Critias.*

The Atlantis Myth has been commonly regarded as an invention of Plato, but it may have a foundation in history: see Appendix, pages 148–9, 158.

HERMOCRATES: I assure you, Socrates, that, as Timaeus here said, there is no lack of willingness on our part and we don't want to excuse ourselves from our part of the bargain. Indeed we were considering it as soon as we got back yesterday to Critias's house, where we are staying, and even before that while we were on the way there. Critias then produced a story he had heard long ago. Tell it again now to Socrates, Critias, so that we can see whether it is suitable for our purpose or not.

CRITIAS: I will, if the other member of the trio, Timaeus, agrees.

TIMAEUS: I agree.

CRITIAS: Listen then, Socrates. The story is a strange one, but Solon, the wisest of the seven wise men, once vouched its truth. He was a relation and close friend of Dropides, my great-grandfather, as he often says himself in his poems, and told the story to my grandfather Critias, who in turn repeated it to us when he was an old man. It relates the many notable achievements of our city long ago, which have been lost sight of because of the lapse of time and destruction of human life. Of these the greatest is one that we could well   21
recall now to repay our debt to you and to offer the Goddess on her festival day a just and truthful hymn of praise.

SOCRATES: Good. And what is this unrecorded yet authentic achievement of our city that Critias heard from Solon and recounted to you?

CRITIAS: I will tell you; though the story was old when I heard it and the man who told it me was no longer young.

For Critias was at the time, so he said, nearly ninety, and I was about ten. It was Children's Day in the festival of Apatouria, and there were the customary ceremonies for the boys, including prizes given by the fathers for reciting. There were recitations of many poems by different authors, but many of the competitors chose Solon's poems, which were in those days quite a novelty. And one of the clansmen, either because he thought so or out of politeness to Critias, said that he thought that Solon was not only the wisest of men but also the most outspoken of poets. And the old man – I remember it well – was extremely pleased, and said with a smile, 'I wish, Amynander, that he hadn't treated poetry as a spare-time occupation but had taken it seriously like others; if he had finished the story he brought back from Egypt, and hadn't been compelled to neglect it because of the class struggles and other evils he found here on his return, I don't think any poet, even Homer or Hesiod, would have been more famous.' 'And what was the story, Critias?' asked Amynander. 'It was about what may fairly be called the greatest and most noteworthy of all this city's achievements, but because of the lapse of time and the death of those who took part in it the story has not lasted till our day.' 'Tell us from the beginning,' came the reply; 'how and from whom did Solon hear the tale which he told you as true?'

'There is in Egypt,' said Critias, 'at the head of the delta, where the Nile divides, a district called the Saïtic. The chief city of the district, from which King Amasis came, is called Saïs. The chief goddess of the inhabitants is called in Egyptian Neïth, in Greek (according to them) Athena; and they are very friendly to the Athenians and claim some relationship to them. Solon came there on his travels and was highly honoured by them, and in the course of making inquiries from those priests who were most knowledgeable on the subject found that both he and all his countrymen were almost entirely ignorant about antiquity. And wishing to lead them on to talk about early times, he embarked on an account of the earliest events known here, telling them about Phoroneus, said to be the first man, and Niobe, and how Deucalion and Pyrrha survived the flood and who were their descendants, and trying by reckoning up the generations to calculate how long ago the events in question had taken place. And a very old priest said to him, 'Oh Solon, Solon, you Greeks are all children, and there's no such thing as an old Greek.'

'What do you mean by that?' inquired Solon.

'You are all young in mind,' came the reply: 'you have no belief rooted in old tradition and no knowledge hoary with age. And the reason is this. There have been and will be many different calamities to destroy mankind, the greatest of them by fire and water, lesser ones by countless other means. Your own story of how Phaëthon, child of the sun, harnessed his father's chariot, but was unable to guide it along his father's course and so burnt up things on the earth and was himself destroyed by a thunderbolt, is a mythical version of the truth that there is at long intervals a variation in the course of the heavenly bodies and a consequent widespread destruction by fire of things on the earth. On such occasions those who live in the mountains or in high and dry places suffer more than those living by rivers or by the sea; as for us, the Nile, our own regular saviour, is freed[1] to preserve us in this emergency. When on the other hand the gods purge the earth with a deluge, the herdsmen and shepherds in the mountains escape, but those living in the cities in your part of the world are swept into the sea by the rivers; here water never falls on the land from above either then or at any other time, but rises up naturally from below. This is the reason why our traditions here are the oldest preserved; though it is true that in all places where excessive cold or heat does not prevent it human beings are always to be found in larger or smaller numbers. But in our temples we have preserved from earliest times a written record of any 23

---

1. The meaning is uncertain, but there may be a reference to Egyptian irrigation systems.

great or splendid achievement or notable event which has come to our ears whether it occurred in your part of the world or here or anywhere else; whereas with you and others, writing and the other necessities of civilization have only just been developed when the periodic scourge of the deluge descends, and spares none but the unlettered and uncultured, so that you have to begin again like children, in complete ignorance of what happened in our part of the world or in yours in early times. So these genealogies of your own people which you were just recounting are little more than children's stories. You remember only one deluge, though there have been many, and you do not know that the finest and best race of men that ever existed lived in your country; you and your fellow citizens are descended from the few survivors that remained, but you know nothing about it because so many succeeding generations left no record in writing. For before the greatest of all destructions by water, Solon, the city that is now Athens was pre-eminent in war and conspicuously the best governed in every way, its achievements and constitution being the finest of any in the world of which we have heard tell.'

Solon was astonished at what he heard and eagerly begged the priests to describe to him in detail the doings of these citizens of the past. 'I will gladly do so, Solon,' replied the priest, 'both for your sake and your city's, but chiefly in gratitude to the Goddess to whom it has fallen to bring up and educate both your country and ours – yours first, when she took over your seed from Earth and Hephaestus, ours a thousand years later. The age of our institutions is given in our sacred records as eight thousand years, and the citizens whose laws and whose finest achievement I will now briefly describe to you therefore lived nine thousand years ago; we will go through their history in detail later on at leisure, when we can consult the records.

'Consider their laws compared with ours; for you will find today among us many parallels to your institutions in those days. First, our priestly class is kept distinct from the

others, as is also our artisan class; next, each class of craftsmen – shepherds, hunters, farmers – performs its function
in isolation from others. And of course you will have
noticed that our soldier class is kept separate from all others,
being forbidden by the law to undertake any duties other
than military: moreover their armament consists of shield
and spear, which we were the first people in Asia to adopt,
under the instruction of the Goddess, as you were in your
part of the world. And again you see what great attention
our law devotes from the beginning to learning, deriving
from the divine principles of cosmology everything needed
for human life down to divination and medicine for our
health, and acquiring all other related branches of knowledge. The Goddess founded this whole order and system
when she framed your society. She chose the place in which
you were born with an eye to its temperate climate, which
would produce men of high intelligence; for being herself a
lover of war and wisdom she picked a place for her first
foundation that would produce men most like herself in
character. So you lived there under the laws I have described,
and even better ones, and excelled all men in every kind of
accomplishment, as one would expect of children and offspring of the gods. And among all the wonderful achievements recorded here of your city, one great act of courage is
outstanding. Our records tell how your city checked a
great power which arrogantly advanced from its base in the
Atlantic ocean to attack the cities of Europe and Asia. For in
those days the Atlantic was navigable. There was an island
opposite the strait which you call (so you say) the Pillars of
Heracles, an island larger than Libya and Asia combined;
from it travellers could in those days reach the other islands, 25
and from them the whole opposite continent which sur-   *America*
rounds what can truly be called the ocean. For the sea
within the strait we were talking about is like a lake with a
narrow entrance; the outer ocean is the real ocean and the
land which entirely surrounds it is properly termed continent. On this island of Atlantis had arisen a powerful and

remarkable dynasty of kings, who ruled the whole island, and many other islands as well and parts of the continent; in addition it controlled, within the strait, Libya up to the borders of Egypt and Europe as far as Tyrrhenia. This dynasty, gathering its whole power together, attempted to enslave, at a single stroke, your country and ours and all the territory within the strait. It was then, Solon, that the power and courage and strength of your city became clear for all men to see. Her bravery and military skill were outstanding; she led an alliance of the Greeks, and then when they deserted her and she was forced to fight alone, after running into direst peril, she overcame the invaders and celebrated a victory; she rescued those not yet enslaved from the slavery threatening them, and she generously freed all others living within the Pillars of Heracles. At a later time there were earthquakes and floods of extraordinary violence, and in a single dreadful day and night all your fighting men were swallowed up by the earth, and the island of Atlantis was similarly swallowed up by the sea and vanished; this is why the sea in that area is to this day impassable to navigation, which is hindered by mud just below the surface,[1] the remains of the sunken island.'

That is, in brief, Socrates, the story which Critias told when he was an old man, and which he had heard from Solon. When you were describing your society and its inhabitants yesterday, I was reminded of this story and noticed with astonishment how closely, by some miraculous chance, your account coincided with Solon's. I was not willing to say so at once, for after so long a time my memory was imperfect; I decided therefore that I must first rehearse the whole story to myself before telling it. That was why I was so quick to agree to your conditions yesterday, thinking that I was pretty well placed to deal with what is always the most serious difficulty in such matters, how to find a suitable story on which to base what one wants to say. And so, as

1. Reading κατὰ βραχέος. Aristotle, *Meteorologica* 354a, 22, mentions 'shallows due to mud' outside the Pillars of Heracles.

Hermocrates said, as soon as we left here yesterday I started telling the story to the others as I remembered it, and when I got back I managed to recall pretty well all of it by thinking it over during the night. It is amazing, as is often said, how what we learn as children sticks in the memory. I'm not at all sure whether I could remember again all I heard yesterday; yet I should be surprised if any detail of this story I heard so long ago has escaped me. I listened to it then with a child's intense delight, and the old man was glad to answer my innumerable questions, so that the details have been indelibly branded on my memory. What is more, I have told the whole story to the others early this morning, so that they might be as well placed as I am for the day's discussion.

And now, to come to the point, I am ready to tell the story, Socrates, not only in outline but in detail, as I heard it. We will transfer the imaginary citizens and city which you described yesterday to the real world, and say that your city is the city of my story and your citizens those historical ancestors of ours whom the priest described. They will fit exactly, and there will be no disharmony if we speak as if they really were the men who lived at that time. We will divide the work between us and try to fulfil your instructions to the best of our ability. So tell us, Socrates, do you think this story will suit our purpose, or must we look for another instead?

SOCRATES: What better choice could there be, Critias? Your story is particularly well suited to the present festival of the Goddess, with whom it is connected, and it is a great point in its favour that it is not a fiction but true history. Where shall we find an alternative if we abandon it? No, you must tell it and good luck to you; and I can take it easy 27 and listen to your reply to my narrative of yesterday.

CRITIAS: Here then, Socrates, is the plan we have made to entertain you. We thought that Timaeus, who knows more about astronomy than the rest of us and who has devoted himself particularly to studying the nature of the universe, should speak first, and starting with the origin of the cosmic system bring the story down to man. I will follow him, assuming that human beings have come into existence as he has described and that some of them have had your excellent education; these I will bring to judgement before us here by making them citizens of Athens governed as she was in the days of Solon's story – an Athens whose disappearance is accounted for in the priestly writings, and about whose citizens I shall in the rest of what I have to say assume I am speaking.

SOCRATES: I look like getting a splendid entertainment in return for mine. It falls to you then, Timaeus, it seems, to speak next, after the customary invocation to the gods.

3. *Prelude. The physical world has only a secondary reality, and knowledge of it is bound to be imprecise.*

TIMAEUS: Yes, Socrates; of course everyone with the least sense always calls on god at the beginning of any undertaking, small or great. So surely, if we are not quite crazy, as we embark on our account of how the universe began, or perhaps had no beginning, we must pray to all the gods and goddesses that what we say will be pleasing to them first, and then to ourselves. Let that be our invocation to the gods: but we must invoke our own powers too, that you may most easily understand and I most clearly expound my thoughts on the subject before us.

We must in my opinion begin by distinguishing between that which always is and never becomes from that which is always becoming but never is. The one is apprehensible by intelligence with the aid of reasoning, being eternally the same, the other is the object of opinion and irrational sensation, coming to be and ceasing to be, but never fully real. In addition, everything that becomes or changes must do so owing to some cause; for nothing can come to be without a cause. Whenever, therefore, the maker of anything keeps

his eye on the eternally unchanging and uses it as his pattern
for the form and function of his product the result must
be good; whenever he looks to something that has come to
be and uses a model that has come to be, the result is not
good.

As for the world – call it that or cosmos or any other name
acceptable to it – we must ask about it the question one is
bound to ask to begin with about anything: whether it has
always existed and had no beginning, or whether it has come
into existence and started from some beginning. The
answer is that it has come into being; for it is visible, tangible, and corporeal, and therefore perceptible by the senses,
and, as we saw, sensible things are objects of opinion and
sensation and therefore change and come into being. And
what comes into being or changes must do so, we said,
owing to some cause. To discover the maker and father of
this universe is indeed a hard task, and having found him it
would be impossible to tell everyone about him. Let us
return to our question, and ask to which pattern did its
constructor work, that which remains the same and un-   29
changing or that which has come to be? If the world is
beautiful and its maker good, clearly he had his eye on the
eternal; if the alternative (which it is blasphemy even to
mention) is true, on that which is subject to change. Clearly,
of course, he had his eye on the eternal; for the world is the
fairest of all things that have come into being and he is the
best of causes. That being so, it must have been constructed
on the pattern of what is apprehensible by reason and understanding and eternally unchanging; from which again it
follows that the world is a likeness of something else. Now
it is always most important to begin at the proper place;
and therefore we must lay it down that the words in which
likeness and pattern are described will be of the same order
as that which they describe. Thus a description of what is
changeless, fixed and clearly intelligible will be changeless
and fixed – will be, that is, as irrefutable and uncontrover-
tible as a description in words can be; but analogously a

description of a likeness of the changeless, being a description of a mere likeness will be merely likely; for being has to becoming the same relation as truth to belief. Don't therefore be surprised, Socrates, if on many matters concerning the gods and the whole world of change we are unable in every respect and on every occasion to render consistent and accurate account. You must be satisfied if our account is as likely as any, remembering that both I and you who are sitting in judgement on it are merely human, and should not look for anything more than a likely story in such matters.

SOCRATES: Certainly, Timaeus; we must accept your principles in full. You have given us a wonderfully acceptable prelude; now go on to develop your main theme.

Main Section I. The work of reason.
4. The motive for creation: the world a unique copy of a unique, perfect and eternal model.

TIMAEUS: Let us therefore state the reason why the framer of this universe of change framed it at all. He was good, and what is good has no particle of envy in it; being therefore without envy he wished all things to be as like himself as possible. This is as valid a principle for the origin of the world of change as we shall discover from the wisdom of men, and we should accept it. God therefore, wishing that all things should be good, and so far as possible nothing be imperfect, and finding the visible universe in a state not of rest but of inharmonious and disorderly motion, reduced it to order from disorder, as he judged that order was in every way better. It is impossible for the best to produce anything but the highest. When he considered, therefore, that in all the realm of visible nature, taking each thing as a whole, nothing without intelligence is to be found that is superior to anything with it, and that intelligence is impossible without soul, in fashioning the universe he implanted reason in soul and soul in body, and so ensured that his work should be by nature highest and best. And so the most likely account must say that this world came to be in very truth, through god's providence, a living being with soul and intelligence.

On this basis we must proceed to the next question: What was the living being in the likeness of which the creator constructed it? We cannot suppose that it was any creature that is part of a larger whole, for nothing can be good that is modelled on something incomplete. So let us assume that it resembles as nearly as possible that of which all other beings individually and generically are parts, and which comprises in itself all intelligible beings, just as this world contains ourselves and all visible creatures. For god's purpose was to use as his model the highest and most completely perfect of intelligible things, and so he created a single visible living being, containing within itself all living beings of the same natural order. Are we then right to speak of one universe, or would it be more correct to speak of a plurality or infinity? ONE is right, if it was manufactured according to its pattern; for that which comprises all intelligible beings cannot have a double. There would have to be another being comprising them both, of which both were parts, and it would be correct to call our world a copy not of them but of the being which comprised them. In order therefore that our universe should resemble the perfect living creature in being unique, the maker did not make two universes or an infinite number, but our universe was and is and will continue to be his only creation.

31

5. *The body of the world. This is composed of four elementary constituents, earth, air, fire and water, the whole available amount of which is used up in its composition. Its shape is spherical and it revolves on its axis.*

Now anything that has come to be must be corporeal,

visible and tangible: but nothing can be visible without
fire, nor tangible without solidity, and nothing can be solid
without earth. So god, when he began to put together the
body of the universe, made it of fire and earth. But it is not
possible to combine two things properly without a third to
act as a bond to hold them together. And the best bond is one
that effects the closest unity between itself and the terms it is
combining; and this is best done by a continued geometrical
proportion. For whenever you have three cube or square
numbers with a middle term such that the first term is to it
32 as it is to the third term, and conversely what the third
term is to the mean the mean is to the first term, then since
the middle becomes first and last and similarly the first and
last become middle, it will follow necessarily that all can
stand in the same relation to each other, and in so doing
achieve unity together.[1] If then the body of the universe
were required to be a plane surface with no depth, one
middle term would have been enough to connect it with the
other terms, but in fact it needs to be solid, and solids always
need two connecting middle terms. So god placed water and
air between fire and earth, and made them so far as possible
proportional to one another, so that air is to water as water
is to earth; and in this way he bound the world into a visible
and tangible whole. So by these means and from these four
constituents the body of the universe was created to be at
unity owing to proportion; in consequence it acquired
concord, so that having once come together in unity with
itself it is indissoluble by any but its compounder.

The construction of the world used up the whole of each
of these four elements. For the creator constructed it of all
the fire and water and air and earth available, leaving over

1. The general algebraic formula is if a:b::b:c, then c:b::b:a and
b:a::c:b. If we ignore the particular qualification 'cube or square
numbers', then 'the sentence simply gives a definition of a continued
geometrical proportion with three terms' (Cornford, p. 45). If we
take (with Cornford) the progression 2, 4, 8 as an illustration, then
2:4::4:8, 8:4::4:2, 4:2::8:4.

no part or property of any of them, his purpose being, firstly, that it should be as complete a living being as possible, a whole of complete parts, and further, that it should be single and there should be nothing left over out of which another such whole could come into being, and finally that it should be ageless and free from disease. For he knew that heat and cold and other things that have powerful effects attack a composite body from without, so causing untimely dissolution, and make it decay by bringing disease and old age upon it. On this account and for this reason he made this world a single complete whole, consisting of parts that are wholes, and subject neither to age nor to disease. The shape he gave it was suitable to its nature. A suitable shape for a living being that was to contain within itself all living beings would be a figure that contains all possible figures within itself. Therefore he turned it into a rounded spherical shape, with the extremes equidistant in all directions from the centre, a figure that has the greatest degree of completeness and uniformity, as he judged uniformity to be incalculably superior to its opposite. And he gave it a perfectly smooth external finish all round, for many reasons. For it had no need of eyes, as there remained nothing visible outside it, nor of hearing, as there remained nothing audible; there was no surrounding air which it needed to breathe in, nor was it in need of any organ by which to take food into itself and discharge it later after digestion. Nothing was taken from it or added to it, for there was nothing that could be; for it was designed to supply its own nourishment from its own decay and to comprise and cause all processes, as its creator thought that it was better for it to be self-sufficient than dependent on anything else. He did not think there was any purpose in providing it with hands as it had no need to grasp anything or defend itself, nor with feet or any other means of support. For of the seven[1] physical

1. The seven motions are: uniform circular motion in the same place, mentioned here, up and down, backwards and forwards, right and left.

34 motions he allotted to it the one which most properly belongs to intelligence and reason, and made it move with a uniform circular motion on the same spot; any deviation into movement of the other six kinds he entirely precluded. And because for its revolution it needed no feet he created it without feet or legs.

This was the plan of the eternal god when he gave to the god about to come into existence a smooth and unbroken surface, equidistant in every direction from the centre, and made it a physical body whole and complete, whose components were also complete physical bodies. And he put soul in the centre and diffused it through the whole and enclosed the body in it. So he established a single spherical universe in circular motion, alone but because of its excellence needing no company other than itself, and satisfied to be its own acquaintance and friend. His creation, then, for all these reasons, was a blessed god.

6. *The soul of the world. The material of the soul is mixed and given the appropriate mathematical structure. It is described as forming a long strip, which is then cut up into narrower strips, which are in turn used to produce the movements of stars and planets. The process has two stages. The material is first cut into two strips, which are placed crosswise and then bent round and made into rings, one, the circle of the Same, for the fixed stars, the other, the circle of the Different, for the planets. The second ring is then subdivided into seven, to allow for sun, moon, and five planets, details of whose movements will be given later* (p. 52). *The world-soul is engaged in a perpetual process of thought about both the sensible and intelligible realm, the circles of Same and Different playing a vital part in that process.*

Three things must be remembered in understanding this section. (1) *That Plato (like all Greeks) believed that all motion must have a cause;* (2) *that the soul, as a self-mover, is for him*

*the ultimate cause of motion; (3) that he held that reasoning
consisted essentially of judgements of sameness (affirmation)
and difference (negation).*

*In writing of the strips or rings that are to carry the planets
Plato probably had in mind, or before him, an astronomical model
of the kind known as an 'armillary sphere' (see frontispiece).*

God did not of course contrive the soul later than the
body, as it has appeared in the narrative we are giving; for
when he put them together he would never have allowed the
older to be controlled by the younger. Our narrative is
bound to reflect much of our own contingent and accidental
state. But god created the soul before the body and gave it
precedence both in time and value, and made it the dominat-
ing and controlling partner. And he composed it in the
following way and out of the following constituents.
From the indivisible, eternally unchanging Existence and   35
the divisible, changing Existence of the physical world he
mixed a third kind of Existence intermediate between them:
again with the Same and the Different he made, in the same
way, compounds intermediate between their indivisible
element and their physical and divisible element: and taking
these three components he mixed them into single unity,
forcing the Different, which was by nature allergic to mixture, into union with the Same, and mixing both with Existence.[1] Having thus made a single whole of these three, he

[1] 'We may set out the full scheme of the Soul's composition as
follows:

First Mixture		*Final Mixture*
Indivisible Existence ⎱	Intermediate ⎱	
Divisible Existence ⎰	Existence	
Indivisible Sameness ⎱	Intermediate ⎱ Soul.'	
Divisible Sameness ⎰	Sameness ⎰	
Indivisible Difference ⎱	Intermediate ⎱	
Divisible Difference ⎰	Difference ⎰	

(Cornford, p. 61).

In 35a, 4, read αὖ πέρι after φύσεως with Cornford.

PLATO

went on to make appropriate subdivisions, each containing
a mixture of Same and Different and Existence. He began
the division as follows. He first marked off a section of the
whole, and then another twice the size of the first; next a
third, half as much again as the second and three times the
first, a fourth twice the size of the second, a fifth three times
36 the third, a sixth eight times the first, a seventh twenty-
seven times the first.[1] Next he filled in the double and treble
intervals by cutting off further sections and inserting them
in the gaps, so that there were two mean terms in each interval, one exceeding one extreme and being exceeded by the
other by the same fraction of the extremes, the other exceeding and being exceeded by the same numerical amount.
These links produced intervals of $\frac{3}{2}$ and $\frac{4}{3}$ and $\frac{9}{8}$ within the
previous intervals, and he went on to fill all intervals of $\frac{4}{3}$
with the interval $\frac{9}{8}$; this left, as a remainder in each, an
interval whose terms bore the numerical ratio of 256 to 243.
And at that stage the mixture from which these sections
were being cut was all used up.[2]

1. The series 1, 2, 3, 4, 9, 8, 27, which, as ancient commentators
pointed out, can be arranged in the following diagram:
In this $4 = 2^2$ and $8 = 2^3$, $9 = 3^2$ and $27 = 3^3$. In Plato's description
the numbers measure off corresponding lengths on a single strip of

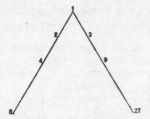

soul-stuff. 4 and 9, 8 and 27 are square and cube numbers which are
thought of as two-dimensional and three-dimensional, planes and
solids. 'The reason for stopping at the cube is that the cube symbolizes
body in three dimensions' (Cornford, p. 68).
2. Plato now treats the intervals which he has marked out on his
soul-stuff as if they defined a musical scale. His primary motive is not

48

He then took the whole fabric and cut it down the middle into two strips, which he placed crosswise at their middle points to form a shape like the letter X; he then bent the ends round in a circle and fastened them to each other opposite the point at which the strips crossed, to make two circles, one inner and one outer. And he endowed them with uniform motion in the same place, and named the movement of the outer circle after the nature of the Same, of the inner after the nature of the Different. The circle of the Same he caused to revolve from left to right, and the circle of the Different from right to left on an axis inclined to it; and made the master revolution that of the Same. For he left the circle of the Same whole and undivided, but slit the inner circle six times to make seven unequal circles, whose intervals were double or triple, three of each; and he made these circles revolve in contrary senses relative to each other, three of them at a similar speed, and four at speeds different from each other and from that of the first three but related proportionately.[1]

---

musical, and though he will later space the seven planets at intervals corresponding to the seven terms, no mention is made of the harmony of the spheres which occurs in the *Republic*. But the knowledge that the relations between the notes of the octave can be numerically expressed had influenced him deeply; he feels that the soul must have some kind of ingrained mathematical structure, and having expressed this in a series of seven numbers, which he will need for other purposes, he then treats the numbers as notes and proceeds to fill in the remaining notes on the resultant scale.

1. For a detailed explanation of this very compressed description see Cornford, p. 80 f. All circles share the movement of the Same (the daily rotation of the fixed stars), but the seven circles or bands of the Different each have an additional motion in a contrary sense, briefly referred to here. The three which revolve at the same speed, which may be regarded as the standard speed of the Different, are the Sun, Venus, and Mercury: the remaining four move at speeds differing from each other and that of the three. The Moon moves in the same sense as the three, but faster than them; the three outer planets, though they move in the same sense, yet move more slowly than the Sun, Venus, and Mercury, and so may be regarded, from another point of view, as moving, at different speeds, in a contrary sense. If I am

And when the whole structure of the soul had been finished to the liking of its framer, he proceeded to fashion the whole corporeal world within it, fitting the two together centre to centre: and the soul was woven right through from the centre to the outermost heaven, which it enveloped from the outside and, revolving on itself, provided a divine source of unending and rational life for all time. The body of the heaven is visible, but the soul invisible and endowed

37 with reason and harmony, being the best creation of the best of intelligible and eternal things. And because it is compounded of Same, Different, and Existence as constituent parts, and divided up and bound together in proportion, and is revolving upon itself, whenever the soul comes in contact with anything whose being is either dispersed or indivisible, it is moved throughout and calculates similarity and difference, that is, in exactly what respect and in what way and how and when it happens that a particular thing is or is qualified by these terms in respect of anything either in the realm of change or in relation to things eternally the same. And whenever reasoning that is true, whether about the different or about the same, takes place, being carried on without speech or sound in the self-moved, if it concerns the sensible world, and the circle of Different, running straight, reports it to the whole soul, then there arise opinions and beliefs that are sure and true: but if it concerns the world apprehended by reason, and the circle of Same, running smoothly, declares it, then the result must be apprehension and knowledge. And if anyone calls that in

---

moving at 2 m.p.h. down the corridor towards the back of a train travelling at 60 m.p.h., then I am moving in the same sense as the train at 58 m.p.h. but still have a motion of my own in a contrary sense to the train. This is the position of the outer planets. The moon is walking down the corridor towards the front.

Plato's expression is extremely condensed, and made still more obscure because he has not yet mentioned the planets to whose movements the sentence refers. The basic principle in his scheme, Pythagorean in origin, is that of explaining the *observed* motions of the Sun, Moon, and planets as the combined result of two or more motions.

which this pair take place anything but soul he is speaking anything but the truth.

7. Time and its measurement. The world cannot be eternal, like its pattern; instead, it exists in time, which is a 'moving image of eternity' and which is measured and defined by the movement of the sun, moon, and planets. These are now created and set in the various orbits, or circles of the Different, described in the previous section.

When the father who had begotten it perceived that the universe was alive and in motion, a shrine for the eternal gods, he was glad, and in his delight planned to make it still more like its pattern; and as this pattern is an eternal Living Being, he set out to make the universe resemble it in this way too as far as was possible. The nature of the Living Being was eternal, and it was not possible to bestow this attribute fully on the created universe; but he determined to make a moving image of eternity, and so when he ordered the heavens he made in that which we call time an eternal moving image of the eternity which remains for ever at one. For before the heavens came into being there were no days or nights or months or years, but he devised and brought them into being at the same time that the heavens were put together; for they are all parts of time, just as past and future are also forms of it, which we wrongly attribute, without thinking, to the Eternal Being. For we say of it that it *was* and *shall be*, but on a true reckoning we should only say *is*, reserving *was* and *shall be* for the process of change in time: for both are motions, but that which is eternally the same and unmoved can neither be becoming older or younger owing to the lapse of time, nor can it ever become so; neither can it now have *become* nor can it come to *be* in the future; nor in general can any of the attributes which becoming attached to sensible and changing things belong to it, for they are all forms of time which in its

38

measurable cycles imitates eternity. Besides, we use such
expressions as what is past *is* past, what is present *is* present,
what is future *is* future, and what is not *is* not, none of which
is strictly accurate, though this is perhaps not a suitable
occasion to go into the question in detail.

So time came into being with the heavens in order that,
having come into being together, they should also be dissolved together if ever they are dissolved; and it was made
as like as possible to eternity, which was its model. For the
model exists eternally and the copy correspondingly has
been and is and will be throughout the whole extent of time.
As a result of this plan and purpose of god for the birth of
time, the sun and moon and the five planets as they are
called came into being to define and preserve the measures of
time. And when he had made a physical body for each of
them, god set the seven of them in the seven orbits of the
circle of the Different. The moon he set in the orbit nearest
the earth, the sun in the next and the morning star and the
one called sacred to Hermes in orbits which they complete in
the same time as the sun does his, but with a power of motion
in a contrary sense to him; consequently the sun, Hermes and
the morning star all alike overtake and are overtaken by each
other.[1] For the rest, if one were to describe in detail where

---

1. There has been much discussion of what is meant by this 'power
of motion in a contrary sense'; see Cornford, p. 106, Taylor, p. 196. If
we look at the astronomical facts, as they were certainly known in
Plato's day, and so, it is fair to presume, known to him, we may say
that the planets have (*a*) a daily motion from east to west; (*b*) a longer-
term motion, against the background of the fixed stars, from west to
east; (*c*) certain motions (including retrogradation) peculiar to each,
their observed motion not being simply the combined result of (*a*) and
(*b*). (*a*) is, as we have seen, accounted for by the Circle of the Same,
(*b*) *in general* by the motion of the Circle of the Different, but there are
variations in the speeds of particular planets (p. 49). In the earlier
passage it was assumed that the Sun, Mercury (Hermes), and Venus
(Morning Star) moved as a group. We are now told that this is not so;
they 'overtake and are overtaken by each other'. 'Venus and Mercury,
though never far from the Sun, sometimes get ahead of him and
appear as morning stars, sometimes drop behind, as evening stars'

god set them and for what reasons, it would involve more attention to a side issue than is justified; the topic is one with which we might deal as it deserves at some later time when we have leisure. Anyhow, when the beings jointly needed for the production of time had been given their appropriate motion and had become living creatures with their bodies bound by the ties of soul, they started to move with the motion of the Different, which traverses that of the Same obliquely and is subject to it,[1] some in larger circles, some in smaller, those with the smaller circles moving faster, those with the larger moving more slowly. And so the movement of the Same caused the bodies which move fastest to appear to be overtaken by those that move most slowly, though they are in fact overtaking them; for because their movements are a combination of two distinct contrary motions, it gave them a spiral twist and made the body which falls behind it most slowly (its own motion being the most rapid of all) seem to keep pace with it most

39

(Cornford, p. 106). They complete their journey through the signs of the Zodiac in a solar year, and in that sense can be grouped with the sun; but they are not always in the same relative positions, 'like a group of racers who reach the goal together, but on the way now one, now another is in front' (Cornford, p. 106). It is this variation of position for which the 'contrary power' is brought into account. And it seems plausible (with Cornford) to regard it as accounting also for the variations of speed already mentioned, and for the retrogradations of the outer planets, whose motions are referred to in the next sentence only to be dismissed. Plato does not mention retrogradation, but he is at pains to emphasize in several places that there are more complications in the planetary movements than he can deal with in the context; Eudoxus, who was working in the Academy at about this time, certainly knew of it, and it seems reasonable to suppose that Plato knew too. We thus get a neat threefold scheme. The Circle of the Same accounts for the daily rotation: the Circle of the Different for the longer-term, west to east, motion: while the 'contrary power' accounts for all differences of speed or other peculiarities. We are told in the next sentence that each planet is a 'living creature', a compound of soul and body (and we shall learn shortly that it is a god); so here again soul is the source of movement.

1. Reading ἰοῦσαν and κρατουμένην, in 39a, 1.

closely.[1] And in the second of the orbits from the earth god lit a light, which we now call the sun, to provide a clear measure of the relative speeds of the eight revolutions,[2] to shine throughout the whole heaven, and to enable the appropriate living creatures to gain a knowledge of number from the uniform movements of the Same. In this way and for this reason there came into being night and day, the period of the single and most intelligent[3] of revolutions; the month, complete when the moon has been round her orbit and caught up the sun again; the year, complete when the sun has been round his orbit. Only a very few men are aware of the periods of the others; they have no name for them and do not calculate their mathematical relationships. They are indeed virtually unaware that their wandering movements are time at all, so bewildering are they in number and so amazing in intricacy. None the less it is perfectly possible to perceive that the perfect temporal number and the perfect year are complete when all eight orbits have reached their total of revolutions relative to each other, measured by the regularly moving orbit of the Same.[4] In this way and for this purpose the stars which turn back in their course through the heavens were made, so that this world should in its imitation of the eternal nature resemble as closely as possible the perfect intelligible Living Creature.

1. This sentence makes two points: (1) That the real movements are not the same as the apparent movements; the moon, for example, which seems to move 'most slowly' is really moving fastest (Cornford, p. 113); (2) that the combination of the motions of Same and Different, which are in different planes, produces a path which if traced on a sphere of the same radius is spiral (Cornford, p. 114). The only connection between the two points seems to be that both contrast apparent and real movements.

2. 39b, 3, read καθ᾽ ἅ.

3. i.e. the movement of the Same.

4. The so-called Great Year, completed when all the heavenly bodies came back to the same relative position.

8. *Living Creatures. There are four kinds of living creature: gods, birds, water animals, land animals. In this part of his account Timaeus deals only with gods, and, among land animals, men. The remainder are dealt with briefly at the end of the dialogue (p.122). (a) There are two kinds of god: (1) the heavenly bodies, which have already largely been dealt with, and the earth; (2) the gods of traditional mythology, for whom we are ironically referred to the traditional sources. Plato certainly held that there are gods other than the heavenly bodies; but he is not prepared to commit himself to detail.*

So far, up to the birth of time, the world's resemblance to its original was complete except in one respect, that all living creatures had as yet not been brought into existence within it. He therefore went on to make it resemble its model in this also. He decided that it should have as many forms of life as intelligence discerns in the perfect Living Creature. There are four of these: the gods in heaven, birds in the air, animals that live in water, and animals that go on dry land. The divine form he made mostly of fire so that it should be as bright and beautiful to look at as possible; and he made it spherical like the universe and set it to follow the movement of the highest intelligence, distributing it round the circle of the heaven to be a kind of universal cosmic embroidery. And he gave each divine being two motions, one uniform in the same place, as each always thinks the same thoughts about the same things, the other forward, as each is subject to the movement of the Same and uniform; but he kept them unaffected by the other five kinds of motion, that each might be as perfect as possible. This is the origin of the fixed stars, which are living beings divine and eternal and remain always rotating in the same place and the same sense; the origin of the planets and their variations, of course, we have already described. And the earth our foster-mother, winding as she does about the axis of the universe,[1]

40

1. The meaning of these words, and in particular the word here

he devised to be the guardian and maker of night and day, and first and oldest of the gods born within the heaven. It would be useless without a visible model to talk about the figures of the dance of these gods, their juxtapositions and the relative counter-revolutions and advances of their orbits, or to describe their conjunctions or oppositions, and how they periodically hide each other from us, disappear and then reappear, causing fear and anxious conjecture about the future to those not able to calculate their movement: so let what we have said be enough and let us conclude our account of the nature of the visible created gods at this point.

It is beyond our powers to know or tell about the birth of the other gods; we must rely on those who have told the story before, who claimed to be children of the gods, and presumably know about their own ancestors. We cannot distrust the children of the gods, even if they give no probable or necessary proof of what they say: we must conform to custom and believe their account of their own family history. Let us therefore follow them in our account of the birth of these gods. Ocean and Tethys were the children of Earth and Heaven, and their children were Phorcys and Cronos and Rhea and their companions; and from Cronos and Rhea were born Zeus and Hera and their brothers and 41 sisters whose names we know, and they in turn had yet further children.

---

translated 'winding' (ἰλλομένην), have been much disputed: see Cornford, p. 120 f., Taylor, p. 226 f. Plato has so far accounted for the apparent movements of the heavenly bodies on the assumption that the earth is at rest at the centre of the universe. And any interpretation of these words must allow for this. Cornford suggests that in order to resist the motion of the Same, which it would otherwise share (the motion of the Different is confined to the sun, moon, and planets), the earth must have a counter-motion of its own, which will exactly cancel it out, and keep the earth at rest without rotation at the centre; and that this is what Plato means to convey by the rather odd word 'winding' (Cornford, p. 120 ff.). This seems the most satisfactory explanation, but Plato can hardly escape the charge of obscurity.

9. Living Creatures. (b) The human soul and body.

Address to the gods, who are to have the task of framing a mortal body for the human soul, which is to be immortal and created by the Demiurge himself.

Anyhow, when all the gods were born, both those whose circuits we see in the sky and those who only appear to us when they wish, the Father of the universe addressed them as follows: 'Ye Gods, those gods whose maker I am and those works whose father I am, being created by me, are indissoluble without my consent.[1] Anything bonded together can of course be dissolved, though only an evil will would consent to dissolve anything whose composition and state were good. Therefore, since you have been created, you are not entirely immortal and indissoluble; but you will never be dissolved nor taste death, as you will find my will a stronger and more sovereign bond than those with which you were bound at your birth. Hear therefore what I now make known to you. There are three kinds of mortal creature yet uncreated, and unless they are created the world will be imperfect, as it will not have in it every kind of living creature which it must have if it is to be perfect. But if these were created and given life by me, they would be equal to gods. In order therefore that there may be mortal creatures and that the whole may be truly a whole, turn your hands, as is natural to you, to the making of living things, taking as your model my own activity in creating you. And in so far as there ought to be something in them that can be named immortal, something called divine, to guide those of them who are ready to follow you and the right, I will begin by sowing the seed of it and then hand it on to you; it remains for you to weave mortal and immortal together and create living creatures. Bring them to birth, give them food and growth, and when they perish receive them again.'

1. 41a, 6, read Θεοὶ, θεῶν ὧν - - - τὰ δι' ἐμοῦ.

10. *The composition and destiny of the human soul. The showing of their destiny to the souls recalls the myth in the* Phaedrus, *the reference to transmigration the myth of Er in the* Republic.

So speaking, he turned again to the same bowl in which he had mixed the soul of the universe and poured into it what was left of the former ingredients, mixing them in much the same fashion as before, only not quite so pure, but in a second and third degree. And when he had compounded the whole, he divided it up into as many souls as there are stars, and allotted each soul to a star. And mounting them on their stars, as if on chariots, he showed them the nature of the universe and told them the laws of their destiny. To ensure fair treatment for each at his hands, the first incarnation would be one and the same for all and each would be sown in its appropriate instrument of time and be born as the most god-fearing of living things; and human-kind being of two sexes, the better of the two was that which in future would be called man. After this necessary incarnation, their body would be subject to physical gain and loss, and they would all inevitably be endowed with the same faculty of sensation dependent on external stimulation, as well as with desire and its mixture of pain and pleasure, and fear and anger with the accompanying feelings and their opposites; mastery of these would lead to a good life, subjection to them to a wicked life. And anyone who lived well for his appointed time would return home to his native star and live an appropriately happy life; but anyone who failed to do so would be changed into a woman at his second birth. And if he still did not refrain from wrong, he would be changed into some animal suitable to his particular kind of wrongdoing, and would have no respite from change and suffering until he allowed the motion of the Same and uniform in himself to subdue all that multitude of riotous and irrational feelings which have clung to it since its assocation with fire, water, air and earth, and with reason thus in control returned once more to his first and best form. Having laid down all these ordinances for them, to avoid being responsible for their subsequent wickednesses he sowed some of them in the earth, some in the moon and some in all the other instruments of time; and what remained to be done after the sowing he left to the newly made gods, who were to fashion mortal bodies and, for the rest, to devise the necessary additions to the human soul and their consequences, and so far as they could control and guide the mortal creature for the best, except, that is, in so far as it became a cause of evil to itself.

11. *The confusion caused by the embodying of the immortal soul in its mortal body. This is expressed in terms of the disordering of the circles of Same and Different; the human soul has been made of the same mixture as the world soul, and therefore has the same structure, though it has mortal additions which will be dealt with later (p. 97).*

Having made all these arrangements, he resumed his accustomed state. Meanwhile, his children remembered and obeyed their father's orders, and took the immortal principle of the mortal creature, and in imitation of their own maker borrowed from the world portions of fire and earth, water and air – loans to be eventually repaid – and welded together what they had borrowed; the bonding they used was not 43 indissoluble, like that by which they were themselves held together, but consisted of a multitude of rivets too small to be seen, which held the part of each individual body together in a unity. And into this body, subject to the flow of growth and decay, they fastened the orbits of the immortal soul. Plunged into this strong stream, the orbits were unable to control it, nor were they controlled by it, and because of the consequent violent conflict the motions of the whole creature were irregular, fortuitous and irrational. It was subject to all six motions, and so strayed in all six directions, backwards and forwards, left and right, up and down. The inward and outward flow of the current which provided it with nourishment was strong; but still greater was the disturbance caused by the properties of objects which it encountered, by the impact of the fire of some external body or of a solid mass of earth, by the liquid flow of water, the sudden blast of driving winds. The motions caused by all these were transmitted through the body and impinged on the soul, and for that reason were later called, as they still are, 'sensations'.[1] At the time of which we are speaking the disturbance was at its greatest, and these motions reinforced the perpetual flow of the body in upsetting the orbits of the soul, bringing that of the Same to a standstill and by their opposition robbing it of power and motion, and disordering that of the Different. The result was that, though the three pairs of intervals of double and triple, and the connecting middle terms of the ratios three to two, four to three, and nine to eight could not be completely dissolved except by him who put them together, they were twisted in all directions and caused every possible kind of shock and damage to the soul's circles, which barely held together, and though they moved, did so quite irregularly, now in reverse, now sideways, now upside down. Something similar happens when a man stands on his head on the ground, pushing his feet against something above him, and what is right and left to him appears reversed to the spectators and vice versa. This and similar effects were produced in the soul's orbits, and when they encountered anything in the category Same or Different in the external world, they made wrong judgements of sameness or difference, and lapsed into falsehood and folly, having no governing orbit in control; for when the impact of external sensation subdues the orbits and their container, then the orbits only seem to be in control but are in fact overpowered. And because of all this the soul when first bound to its mortal body is as much without

1. 'Sensation', αἴσθησις, is here supposed to be derived from ἀίσσω, a verb meaning 'rapid movement'.

reason today as it was in the beginning. But when the stream of growth and nourishment flows less strongly, the soul's orbits take advantage of the calm and as time passes steady down in their proper courses, and the movement of the circles at last regains its correct natural form, and they can name the Different and the Same correctly and render their possessor rational. And if at this stage education is added to correct nurture, a man becomes altogether sound and healthy and avoids the deadliest disease; but if he is careless, after limping through life he returns again to Hades in unregenerate folly. But that is a later stage; our present topic still needs closer investigation, and we must proceed to give as likely an account as we can of its preliminaries, and tell how body and soul were created part by part by the agency and providence of the gods.

12. *The human body: head and limbs.*

They copied the shape of the universe and fastened the two divine orbits of the soul into a spherical body, which we now call the head, the divinest part of us which controls all the rest; they then put together the body as a whole to serve the head, knowing that it would be endowed with all the varieties of motion there were to be. And to prevent the head from rolling about on the earth, unable to get over or out of its many heights and hollows, they provided that the body should act as a convenient vehicle. It was therefore given height and grew four limbs which could bend and stretch, and with which it could take hold of things and support itself, and so by god's contrivance move in all directions carrying on top of it the seat of our divinest and holiest part. That is the reason why we all have arms and legs. And as the gods hold that the front is more honourable and commanding than the back, they made us move, for the most part, forwards. So it was necessary to distinguish the front of man's body and make it different from the back; 45

and to do this they placed the face on this side of the sphere of the head, and fixed in it organs for the soul's forethought, and arranged that this our natural front should take the lead.

13. *The eyes and the mechanism of vision: sleep and dreams: note on mirror-images. For Plato the mechanism of sight involves three kinds of 'fire' or light.* (1) *Daylight, diffused by the sun;* (2) *a visual current, the same in kind as daylight, which is contained in the eye and is directed from it towards the object seen;* (3) *'fire' or light which streams off the body seen, joins the visual ray, and produces effects which result in colour-vision.* (3) *is dealt with more fully later when Plato discusses colour (p. 94).*

And the first organs they fashioned were those that give us light, which they fastened there in the following way. They arranged that all fire which had not the property of burning, but gave out a gentle light, should form the body of each day's light. The pure fire within us that is akin to this they caused to flow through the eyes, making the whole eye-ball, and particularly its central part, smooth and close-textured so that it would keep in anything of coarser nature, and filter through only this pure fire. So when there is daylight round the visual stream, it falls on its like and coalesces with it, forming a single uniform body in the line of sight, along which the stream from within strikes the external object. Because the stream and daylight are similar, the whole so formed is homogeneous, and the motions caused by the stream coming into contact with an object or an object coming into contact with the stream penetrate right through the body and produce in the soul the sensation which we call sight. But when the kindred fire disappears at nightfall, the visual stream is cut off; for what it encounters is unlike itself and so it is changed and quenched, finding nothing with which it can coalesce in the surrounding air which contains no fire. It ceases therefore to see and induces sleep. For when the eyelids, designed by the gods to protect the sight, are shut, they confine the activity of the fire within, and this smoothes and diffuses the internal motions, and produces a calm; when this calm is profound the resultant sleep has few dreams, but when rather more motion remains images, corresponding in quality and number to the type and location of the residual motions, are formed 46 internally and remembered as external events when we wake.[1] And the principles governing reflections in mirrors[2]

1. Or 'remembered when we have emerged into the waking world'.
2. This note on mirror-images seems oddly out of place to the modern reader. But, as Cornford points out, metaphors from vision are common in Plato. In the *Republic* there is the sun simile, with its comparison between eye and sun on the one hand and mind and truth on the other, and the Divided Line whose lowest section contained *images*; in the *Timaeus* the visible world is an *image* of an intelligible model, in the *Sophist* the sophist is an *image* maker. The contrast between image and reality is in fact a recurrent theme throughout Plato's writings, and this may well have diverted him at this point to an account of the images seen in the physical process of reflection.

Again the account is very compressed, but what happens with a normal mirror-image may be roughly represented as follows:

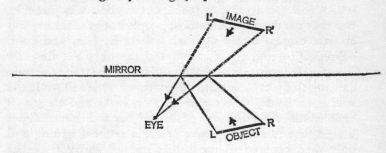

FIGURE I

The example given of an object is the human face – Plato is thinking of looking at oneself in a mirror. When the mirror is concave the rays change sides, and if it is turned through a right angle the image appears upside-down. It is not easy to see how either process takes place, but Plato's knowledge of optics was elementary.

and other smooth reflecting surfaces are not difficult to understand. All such appearances are necessary consequences of the combination of the internal and external fire, which form a unity at the reflecting surface, though distorted in various ways, the fire of the face seen coalescing with that of the eye on the smooth reflecting surface. And the right-hand side appears as the left in the image because reverse parts of the visual stream are in contact with reverse parts of the object as compared with what happens in normal vision. On the other hand, right appears as right and left as left when the visual stream is reversed at the point of coalescence, as when the surface of a mirror is concave and transfers the right side of the visual stream to the left and the left to the right. The same mirror turned lengthwise again, makes the face appear upside down, turning the ray top to bottom.

14. *The distinction between subordinate accessory causes and intelligent purpose, illustrated by the examples of sight and hearing.*

All these are among the subordinate accessory causes which god uses in shaping things in the best way possible. But they are thought of by most people not as accessory but as true causes, achieving their effects by heat and cold, solidification and liquefaction, and the like. Yet they are completely incapable of reason or intelligence; for the only existing thing capable of intelligence we must call soul, and soul is invisible, whereas fire, water, earth and air are all visible bodies. So the lover of intelligence and knowledge is bound first to investigate causes of a rational nature, and only then proceed to those that operate through bodies whose motion is derived from others and must be passed on to others. Our procedure must be the same. We must deal with causes of both sorts, keeping those that operate intelligently and produce results that are good separate from those that operate without reason and produce effects which are casual and random. As far as the eyes are concerned, we have said enough about the accessory causes which give them the powers they now possess; we must go on to describe the chief benefit of the function of sight, which was god's reason for giving it to us. For I reckon that the 47 supreme benefit for which sight is responsible is that not a word of all we have said about the universe could have been said if we had not seen stars and sun and heaven. As it is, the sight of day and night, the months and returning years, the equinoxes and solstices, has caused the invention of number, given us the notion of time, and made us inquire into the nature of the universe; thence we have derived philosophy, the greatest gift the gods have ever given or will give to mortals. This is what I call the greatest good our eyes give us. There is no need to recite the lesser goods, which anyone who was not a philosopher and had lost his sight might lament in vain; let us rather say that the cause and purpose of god's invention and gift to us of sight was that we should see the revolutions of intelligence in the heavens and use their untroubled course to .guide the troubled revolutions in our own understanding, which are akin to them, and so, by learning what they are and how to calculate them accurately according to their nature, correct the disorder of our own revolutions by the standard of the invariability of those of god. The same applies again to sound and hearing, which were given by the gods for the same end and purpose. Speech was directed to just this end to which it makes an outstanding contribution; and all audible musical sound[1] is given us for the sake of harmony, which has motions akin to the orbits in our soul, and which, as anyone who makes intelligent use of the arts knows, is not to be used, as is commonly thought, to give irrational pleasure, but as a heaven-sent ally in reducing to order and harmony any disharmony in the revolutions within us. Rhythm, again, was given us from the same heavenly source to help us in the same way; for most of us lack measure and grace.

1. 47d, 1, read φωνῆς.

Main Section II. The work of necessity.
15. *The world is the product not of reason alone, but of the combination of reason and necessity. We must therefore make a fresh start and examine the working of necessity, the indeterminate cause.*

In almost all we have said we have been describing the products of intelligence; but beside reason we must also set the results of necessity. For this world came into being from a mixture and combination of necessity and intelligence. Intelligence controlled necessity by persuading it for the most part to bring about the best result, and it was by this subordination of necessity to reasonable persuasion that the universe was originally constituted as it is. So that to give a true account of how it came to be on these principles, one must bring in the indeterminate cause[1] so far as its nature permits.[2] We must therefore retrace our steps, and find another suitable original principle for this part of our story, and begin again from the beginning as we did before. We must, that is, consider what was the nature of fire, water, earth and air before the beginning of the world and what their state was then. For no one has yet explained their origin, but we talk as if people knew what fire and each of the others are, and treat them as the alphabet of the universe, whereas they ought not really to be compared even to syllables by anyone with the least sense. Our own position may therefore be defined as follows. It is not for us to describe the original principle or principles (call them what you will) of the universe, for the simple reason that it would be difficult to explain our views in the context of this discussion. You must not therefore expect such a description from me, nor could I persuade myself that I was right

1. More usually translated 'errant cause'. The literal meaning of the Greek word is 'wandering', and there is an implied contrast between something whose course is regular and predictable and something which 'wanders' irregularly and so unpredictably.
2. Or 'and how it is a natural source of motion'.

to undertake a task of such magnitude. I shall stick to the principle of likelihood which I laid down at the start, and try to give an account of everything in detail from the beginning that will be more rather than less likely.[1] So let us begin again, calling as we do so on some protecting deity to see us safely through a strange and unusual argument to a likely conclusion.

16. *The receptacle of becoming.*

We must start our new description of the universe by making a fuller subdivision than we did before; we then distinguished two forms of reality – we must now add a third. Two were enough at an earlier stage, when we postulated on the one hand an intelligible and unchanging model and on the other a visible and changing copy of it. We did not distinguish a third form, considering two would be enough; but now the argument compels us to try to describe in words a form that is difficult and obscure. What must we suppose its powers and nature to be? In general terms, it is the receptacle and, as it were, the nurse of all becoming and change. But true as this is, it needs a great deal of further clarification, and that is difficult, among other reasons, because it requires a preliminary discussion about fire and the other elements.

49

17. *The names fire, air, water, earth really indicate differences of quality not of substance.*

For it is difficult to say with complete certainty which of the elements we really ought to call water rather than fire, or indeed which we ought to call by any name rather than by another or even by all four. How then and in what terms can

1. Omitting καὶ ἔμπροσθεν 48d, 3.

we reasonably express our difficulty? Let us begin with what we now call water. We see it, as we suppose, solidifying into stones and earth, and again dissolving and evaporating into wind and air; air by combustion becomes fire, and fire in turn when extinguished and condensed takes the form of air again; air contracts and condenses into cloud and mist, and these when still more closely compacted become running water, which again turns into earth and stones. There is in fact a process of cyclical transformation. Since therefore none of them ever appears constantly under the same form, it would be embarrassing to maintain that any of them is certainly one rather than another. On the contrary, we shall be safest if we speak about them on the following assumptions. Whenever we see anything in process of change, for example fire, we should speak of it not as *being a thing* but as *having a quality*;[1] water, again we should speak of not as a *thing* but as *having a quality*. And in general we should never speak as if any of the things we suppose we can indicate by pointing and using the expressions 'this thing' or 'that thing' have any permanent reality: for they have no stability and elude the designation 'this' or 'that' or any other that expresses permanence.[2] We should not use these expressions of them, but in each and every case speak of a continually recurrent similar quality. Thus we should give the name fire to one uniformly occurring quality, and so on for everything else in process of change. We should only use the expression 'this thing' or 'that thing' when speaking of that in which this process takes place and in which these qualities appear for a time and then vanish; we should never apply them to any quality, to hot or cold, for example, or any other contraries, or to any derivation of them.

1. Omitting πῦρ 49d, 6.
2. Omitting καὶ τὴν τῷδε in 49e, 3.
Plato is contrasting a Greek word which means 'this' or 'that', and indicates that we are talking of a permanent *thing*, with another which means 'suchlike' or 'having a quality'.

18. *The receptacle compared to a mass of plastic material upon which differing impressions are stamped. As such it has no definite character of its own.*

Let me try to explain the point again more clearly. Suppose a man modelling geometrical shapes of every kind in gold, and constantly remoulding each shape into another. If anyone were to point to one of them and ask what it was it would be much the safest, if we wanted to tell the truth, to say that it was gold and not to speak of the triangles and other figures as being real things, because they would be changing as we spoke; we should be content if they even admit of a qualitative[1] description with any certainty. The same argument applies to the natural receptacle of all bodies. It can always be called the same because it never alters its characteristics. For it continues to receive all things, and never itself takes a permanent impress from any of the things that enter it; it is a kind of neutral plastic material on which changing impressions are stamped by the things which enter it, making it appear different at different times. And the things which pass in and out of it are copies of the eternal realities, whose form they take in a wonderful way that is hard to describe – we will follow this up some other time. For the moment we must make a threefold distinction and think of that which becomes, that in which it becomes, and the model which it resembles. We may indeed use the metaphor of birth and compare the receptacle to the mother, the model to the father, and what they produce between them to their offspring; and we may notice that, if an imprint is to present a very complex appearance, the material on which it is to be stamped will not have been properly prepared unless it is devoid of all the characters which it is to receive. For if it were like any of the things that enter it, it would badly distort any impression of a contrary or entirely different nature when it received it, as its own features would shine through. So anything that is to receive in it-

1. i.e. 'triangular', etc.

69

self every kind of character must be devoid of all character. Manufacturers of scent contrive the same initial conditions when they make liquids which are to receive the scent as odourless as possible: and those who set about making impressions in some soft substance, make its surface as smooth as possible and allow no impression at all to remain visible in it. In the same way that which is going to receive properly and uniformly all the likenesses of the intelligible and eternal things must itself be devoid of all character.[1] Therefore we must not call the mother and receptacle of visible and sensible things either earth or air or fire or water, nor yet any of their compounds or components; but we shall not be wrong if we describe it as invisible and formless, all-embracing, possessed in a most puzzling way of intelligibility, yet very hard to grasp. And so far as we can arrive at its nature from what we have said, the most accurate description would be to say that the part of it which has become fiery appears as fire, the part which has become wet appears as water, and other parts appear as earth and air in so far as they respectively come to resemble them.

19. *The originals on which the qualities of fire, air, etc., which appear in the receptacle, are modelled are the forms, which exist 'in themselves' and whose reality is guaranteed by the difference between opinion and intellectual knowledge.*

But our inquiry needs closer logical definition. Is there such a thing as 'fire in itself', and do all these other realities of which we use this phrase 'so-and-so in itself' exist? Or are the things we see and perceive by our other senses the only true realities? Is there nothing besides them and are we talking nonsense when we say there are intelligible forms of particular things? Is this merely an empty expression? We

1. Reading τῷ τὰ πάντα τῶν νοητῶν 51a, 1.

ought not to dismiss the issue without trial or examination simply by saying that it is so; nor ought we to embark on a long digression in an already long argument. The most suitable procedure would be to make the important distinction in a few words; and so this is how I deliver my verdict. If intelligence and true opinion are different in kind, then these 'things-in-themselves' certainly exist, forms imperceptible to our senses, but apprehended by thought; but if, as some think, there is no difference between true opinion and intelligence, what we perceive through our physical senses must be taken as the most certain reality. Now there is no doubt that the two are different, because they differ in origin and nature. One is produced by teaching, the other by persuasion; one always involves truth and rational argument, the other is irrational; one cannot be moved by persuasion, the other can; true opinion is a faculty shared, it must be admitted, by all men, intelligence by the gods and only a small number of men.

20. *Summary description of the three factors, Form, Copy and Receptacle, which is now called Space.*

If this is so, it must be agreed that there exist, first, the 52 unchanging form, uncreated and indestructible, admitting no modification and entering no combination, imperceptible to sight or the other senses, the object of thought: second, that which bears the same name as the form and resembles it, but is sensible, has come into existence, is in constant motion, comes into existence in and vanishes from a particular place, and is apprehended by opinion with the aid of sensation: third, space which is eternal and indestructible, which provides a position for everything that comes to be, and which is apprehended without the senses by a sort of spurious reasoning and so is hard to believe in – we look at it indeed in a kind of dream and say that everything that exists must be somewhere and occupy some space, and that what is nowhere in heaven or earth is nothing at all. And because of this dream state we are not awake to the distinctions we have drawn and others akin to them, and fail to state the truth about the true and unsleeping reality: namely that whereas an image, the terms of whose existence are outside its control in that it is always a moving shadow of something else, needs to come into existence in something else if it is to claim some degree of reality, or else be nothing at all, an exact and true account of what is ultimately real supports the view that so long as two things are different neither will come to be in the other and so become at once both one and two.

21. *Description of the primitive chaos.*

My verdict, in short, may be stated as follows. There were, before the world came into existence, being, space, and becoming, three distinct realities. The nurse of becoming was characterized by the qualities of water and fire, of earth and air, and by others that go with them, and its visual appearance was therefore varied; but as there was no homogeneity or balance in the forces that filled it, no part of it was in equilibrium, but it swayed unevenly under the impact of their motion, and in turn communicated its motion to them. And its contents were in constant process of movement and separation, rather like the contents of a winnowing basket or similar implement for cleaning corn, in which the solid and heavy stuff is sifted out and settles on one side, the light and insubstantial on another: so the four basic constituents were shaken by the receptacle, which acted as a kind of shaking implement, and those most like each other pushed together most closely, with the result that they came to occupy different regions of space even before they were arranged into an ordered universe. Before that time they were all without proportion or measure; fire, water, earth and air bore some traces of their proper nature, but were in the disorganized state to be expected of anything which god has not touched, and his first step when he set about reducing them to order was to give them a definite pattern of shape and number. We must thus assume as a principle in all we say that god brought them to a state of the greatest possible perfection, in which they were not before. Our immediate task is to attempt an explanation of the particular structure and origin of each; its terms will be unfamiliar, but you will be able to follow as you have been trained in the branches of knowledge which it must employ.

22. *The four elements and the regular solids. Geometrically, solids are bounded by planes, and the most elementary plane figure is the triangle. Two types of triangle are chosen as the basic constituents of all solid bodies, and four basic solids are constructed from them. Transformation of the elements one into another is accounted for by three of them being built up from the same type of basic triangle: the fourth (earth) being built up from triangles of the other type cannot be transformed into the remaining three.*

In the first place it is clear to everyone that fire, earth, water and air are bodies, and all bodies are solids. All solids again are bounded by surfaces, and all rectilinear surfaces are composed of triangles. There are two basic types of triangle, each having one right angle and two acute angles: in one of them these two angles are both half right angles, being subtended by equal sides, in the other they are unequal, being subtended by unequal sides. This we postulate as the origin of fire and the other bodies, our argument combining likelihood and necessity; their more ultimate origins are known to god and to men whom god loves. We must proceed to inquire what are the four most perfect possible bodies which, though unlike one another, are some of them capable of transformation into each other

73

on resolution. If we can find the answer to this question we have the truth about the origin of earth and fire and the two mean terms between them; for we will never admit that there are more perfect visible bodies than these, each in its type. So we must do our best to construct four types of perfect body and maintain that we have grasped their nature sufficiently for our purpose. Of the two basic triangles, then, the isosceles has only one variety, the scalene an infinite number. We must therefore choose, if we are to start according to our own principles, the most perfect of this infinite number. If anyone can tell us of a better choice of triangle for the construction of the four bodies, his criticism will be welcome; but for our part we propose to pass over all the rest and pick on a single type, that of which a pair compose an equilateral triangle. It would be too long a story to give the reason, but if anyone can produce a proof that it is not so we will welcome his achievement.[1] So let us

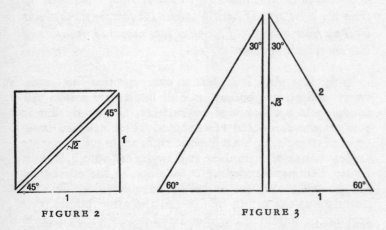

FIGURE 2   FIGURE 3

The two basic triangles. Cornford suggests that their selection is determined by 'the choice of the regular solids' for the four elements; but there is an interesting alternative suggestion in Toulmin and Goodfield, *The Architecture of Matter* (Penguin Books), p. 80.

1. Reading μὴ 54b, 2.

assume that these are the two triangles from which fire and the other bodies are constructed, one isosceles and the other having a greater side whose square is three times that of the lesser. We must now proceed to clarify something we left undetermined a moment ago. It appeared as if all four types of body could pass into each other in the process of change; but this appearance is misleading. For, of the four bodies that are produced by our chosen types of triangle, three are composed of the scalene, but the fourth alone from the isosceles. Hence all four cannot pass into each other on resolution, with a large number of smaller constituents forming a lesser number of bigger bodies and vice versa; this can only happen with three of them. For these are all composed of one triangle, and when larger bodies are broken up a number of small bodies are formed of the same constituents, taking on their appropriate figures; and when small bodies are broken up into their component triangles a single new larger figure may be formed as they are unified into a single solid.[1]

So much for their transformation into each other. We must next describe what geometrical figure each body has and what is the number of its components. We will begin with the construction of the simplest and smallest figure. Its basic unit is the triangle whose hypotenuse is twice the length of its shorter side. If two of these are put together with the hypotenuse as diameter of the resulting figure, and if the process is repeated three times and the diameters and

1. The three sentences are very compressed and to some extent anticipate what we shall shortly be told about the distribution of regular solids between the elements. The process of transformation is thought of as the breaking down of a regular solid into its constituent triangles, which can then rejoin to form a solid of different figure. From this process the cube (earth) must be excluded as its constituent triangle is of a different type to that of the other three. The description of the process of transformation is somewhat obscure but will be elaborated later.

The exclusion of earth from the cycle of transformation seems to be due solely to the assignation to it of the cube, and not to be based on any facts of observation.

shorter sides of the three figures are made to coincide in the same vertex, the result is a single equilateral triangle composed of six basic units. And if four equilateral triangles are put together, three of their plane angles meet to form a single solid angle, the one which comes next after the most obtuse of plane angles:[1] and when four such angles have been formed the result is the simplest solid figure, which divides the surface of the sphere circumscribing it into equal and similar parts.

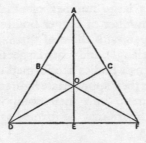

FIGURE 4

'Two of these': e.g. ABO, ACO. 'The resulting figure': e.g. ABOC. The three figures ABOC, DBOE, FEOC coincide at the same vertex O and produce the equilateral triangle ADF.

The second figure is composed of the same basic triangles put together to form eight equilateral triangles, which yield a single solid angle from four planes. The formation of six such solid angles completes the second figure.

The third figure is put together from one hundred and twenty basic triangles, and has twelve solid angles, each bounded by five equilateral plane triangles, and twenty faces, each of which is an equilateral triangle.

After the production of these three figures the first of our

1. The triangles are equilateral, so each solid angle contains $3 \times 60°$ = 180°: the phrase 'the one which comes next after . . .' means the 'least angle which is not less than 180°', another way of saying it is itself 180° (Taylor, p. 375).

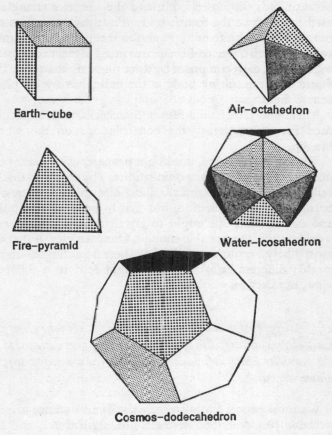

Earth–cube

Air–octahedron

Fire–pyramid

Water–icosahedron

Cosmos–dodecahedron

FIGURE 5

The four figures are the pyramid, the octahedron, the icosahedron, and the cube; the fifth the dodecahedron. The dodecahedron cannot be constructed out of the basic triangles, and because it approaches the sphere most nearly in volume is associated here with 'the whole (spherical) heaven', just as it is associated in the *Phaedo* 110b with the spherical earth. Just how Plato supposed god used it for 'embroidering the constellations on the heavens' we are not told. The Greek word means embroidering or drawing figures of living creatures and of course many constellations are named after divine, human or animal figures.

basic units is dispensed with, and the isosceles triangle is used to produce the fourth body. Four such triangles are put together with their right angles meeting at a common vertex to form a square. Six squares fitted together complete solid angles, each composed by three plane right angles. The figure of the resulting body is the cube, having six plane square faces.

There still remained a fifth construction, which the god used for embroidering the constellations on the whole heaven.

With all this in mind, one might properly ask whether the number of worlds is finite or indefinite. The answer is that to call it indefinite is to express an indefinite opinion where one needs definite information, but that to pause at this point and ask whether one ought to say that there is really one world or five is reasonable enough. Our own view is that the most likely account reveals that there is a single, divine world; different considerations might lead to a different view, but they may be dismissed.[1]

23. *Assignment of the four regular solids to the four elements. Each element is composed of particles of the figure assigned to it, the particles being individually invisible (as we might say, of atomic size).*

We must proceed to distribute the figures whose origins we have just described between fire, earth water, and air. Let us assign the cube to earth; for it is the most immobile of the four bodies and the most retentive of shape, and these are characteristics that must belong to the figure with the most stable faces. And of the basic triangles we have assumed, the isosceles has a naturally more stable base than the scalene, and of the equilateral figures composed of them the square

1. The 'fifth construction' has been mentioned almost as an after-thought, and this paragraph seems to be a footnote suggested by it. Its point and precise meaning are obscure.

is, in whole and in part, a firmer base than the equilateral 56
triangle. So we maintain our principle of likelihood by
assigning it to earth, while similarly we assign the least
mobile of the other figures to water, the most mobile to
fire, and the intermediate to air. And again we assign the
smallest figure to fire, the largest to water, the intermediate
to air; the sharpest to fire, the next sharpest to air, and the
least sharp to water. So to sum up, the figure which has the
fewest faces must in the nature of things be the most mobile,
as well as the sharpest and most penetrating, and finally,
being composed of the smallest number of similar parts,
the lightest. Our second figure will be second in all these
respects, our third will be third. Logic and likelihood thus
both require us to regard the pyramid as the solid figure that
is the basic unit or seed of fire; and we may regard the second
of the figures we constructed as the basic unit of air, the
third of water. We must, of course, think of the individual
units of all four bodies as being far too small to be visible,
and only becoming visible when massed together in large
numbers; and we must assume that the god duly adjusted
the proportions between their numbers, their movements,
and their other qualities and brought them in every way to
the exactest perfection permitted by the willing consent of
necessity.

24. *The process of transformation further explained. The
main bulk of each element tends to collect in a particular
region.*

From all we have so far said about the four basic constituents their behaviour is most likely to be as follows.[1] When
earth meets fire it will be dissolved by its sharpness, and,
whether dissolution takes place in fire itself or in a mass of
air or water, will drift about until its parts meet, fit together
and become earth again; for they can never be transformed

1. Reading ὧν περὶ 57c, 8.

into another figure. But when water is broken up by fire or again by air, its parts can combine to make one of fire and two of air; and the fragments of a single particle of air can make two of fire.[1] Again, when a little fire is enveloped in a large mass of air or water or earth and continues its motion in the moving mass, its resistance is overcome and it is broken up, and two particles of fire combine to make a single figure of air; and when air is forcibly broken up two and a half of its figures will unite to make up a single figure of water. In fact we may restate the matter as follows: I. When one of the other three is surrounded by fire and cut up by the sharpness of its angles and edges, (a) the process is halted if it is reconstituted into fire as none of them can effect any change in or suffer any change from what is similar to and identical in character with itself; (b) but the process of dissolution continues so long as transformation produces a weaker mass to offer resistance to a stronger one. II. On the other hand a few smaller particles when surrounded by a mass of larger ones are broken up and extinguished, and (a) the process of extinction ceases if they are prepared to merge into the figure of the predominant mass, when fire turns into air, air into water; (b) but if while they are so merging one of the other basic constituents comes in conflict with them,[2] dissolution goes on until they are either dispersed to their like after complete dissolution under pressure or else mastered and forced to unite with the predominant mass, take on its character and combine with it. It should be added that during the process they all change their places; for owing to the motion of the receptacle the main bulk of each constituent collects in its own separate place, while any part of it which loses its own form and

1. This sentence gives the most precise formulation of the process by which one element changes into another. Using W, A, F for water, air and fire, we can say:

$W = F+2A$, because in terms of basic triangles, $40 = (2\times16)+8$.
$A = 2F$, because in terms of basic triangles, $16 = 2\times8$.

2. Reading ἐὰν δ'εἰς ταῦτα ἴῃ.

takes on another's is drawn by the shaking to the place of the one whose form it has taken.

25. *The basic triangles are of more than one size, which accounts for the variety of forms taken by the four elements.*

Plato commonly uses a word for his elements which means 'kind' or 'genus'. So e.g. earth is thought of as including all solids, water as including all liquids. Variety in the size of the triangles is introduced to account for this variety within the elements.

The precise interpretation of the passage is not easy, and the reader is referred to Cornford, p. 23c ff.

These are the causes of the formation of the pure primary bodies. The presence in each kind of further varieties is due to the construction of the two basic triangles. This originally produced triangles not in one size only, but some smaller and some larger, the number of sizes corresponding to the number of varieties. So their combinations with themselves and with each other give rise to endless complexities, which anyone who is to give a likely account of reality must survey.

26. *Motion and rest are due to disequilibrium between the four elements, which causes the process of transformation between the elements (which form a continuum shut in and contained by the sphere of the heavens) to continue unceasingly.*

We must also reach agreement about the manner and conditions in which motion and rest arise if the course of our subsequent reasoning is to be clear. We have already said something about them, but must now add that motion can never take place in conditions of uniformity. For it is difficult, or rather impossible, for what is moved to exist without what causes its motion, or what is to cause motion without that which is to be moved; without them there can be no motion and they cannot be in equilibrium. So we must assume that rest and equilibrium are always associated, motion and 58 equilibrium always dissociated; and the cause of disequilibrium is inequality, whose origin we have already described.[1] What we have not explained is how each constituent body has not been entirely separated off from the others and so brought mutual change and interpenetration to an end. The explanation is as follows. The circuit of the whole, within which the constituents are comprised, being spherical and therefore naturally inclined to return on itself, hems them in and allows no space to remain empty. So fire has achieved the maximum interpenetration of the rest; air the second, having the second finest particles; and so on with the others. For those with the largest particles leave the largest gaps in their texture, and those with the smallest the smallest. So the contraction involved in process of compression forces the small particles into the gaps left between the large ones. You thus have a process in which small particles are juxtaposed with large ones, and the smaller disintegrate the larger while the larger cause the smaller to combine, and all are carried, up or down, to their own region; for a change in size involves a change in the position of their region. In this way a constant disequilibrium is maintained which ensures that the perpetual motion of the constituents shall continue unceasingly.

1. There was no equilibrium in the original chaos (p. 72), and the account of the transformation of the elements just given has merely described more precisely the processes of change which result. We are now told that though each element tends to collect together on its own, no final separation is possible because they are all hemmed in by the sphere of the heavens within which they form a continuum as there is no void.

Varieties and compounds of the four primary bodies. Plato has already (p. 81) made provision for varieties in the four elements, and he now proceeds to describe some of them, together with some compounds of more than one element.[1]

27. (a) *He starts with a brief section on fire and air.*

Next we must notice that there are several kinds of *fire*: flame; the radiation from flame which does not burn but provides the eyes with light; and the glow left in embers after flame has been quenched. So again with *air*: there is the brightest variety which we call aether, the muddiest which we call mist and darkness, and other kinds for which we have no name, but which are produced by the unequal sizes of the triangles.

28. (b) *Water, liquid and 'fusible' (e.g. metals).*

There are two main types of *water*: (1) the liquid and (2) the fusible.

(1) The liquid is composed of small and unequal basic units, and so is inherently mobile and easily set in motion by something else because of its lack of uniformity and the shape of its figure.

(2) The fusible type is composed of large and uniform basic units and is therefore more stable and solidified by its uniformity. But fire penetrates and dissolves it and makes it lose its uniformity, and in consequence become more mobile; in that state the pressure of the neighbouring air makes it

1. Plato is not very precise in this and the next sections (28–30), but he has made the following provision for variety: (1) The four basic *shapes* of particles account in general for the differences between the four elements. (2) Differences in the *size* of particles account for particular *varieties* of the elements – e.g. types of fire (27a) and water (28b). (3) There are substances in which the particles are all of the same *shape* but differ in *size* (e.g. copper, p. 84). Finally there are substances which contain more than one *element* or *variety* of element (e.g. 'juices', which contain water and fire).

59 spread over the ground. The breakdown of uniformity in the particles is called melting, and the spreading over the ground flowing. In the reverse process the fire escapes, but as it does not pass into a vacuum compresses the neighbouring air which in turn compresses the liquid mass, still in a plastic state, into the space left by the fire and makes it homogeneous. Under pressure the mass regains its uniformity, which had been upset by the escaping fire, and settles into its original state. And the loss of fire is called cooling, and the contraction which follows is called a state of solidity.

Of all these fusible varieties of water, as we have called them, *gold* is unique in quality and most highly valued. It is very dense, being compounded of very fine and uniform particles, in colour it is yellow and gleaming, and it solidifies after being filtered through rock. The scion of gold, which is very hard because of its density and dark in colour, is called *adamant*.[1]

Another variety has particles like gold, but of more than one size: it is denser than gold and has a small admixture of fine earth which makes it harder; on the other hand it is lighter because it has large interstices in it. This formation is *copper*, one of the bright and solidified varieties of water. The admixture of earth, when the two separate in course of time, appears on the surface of the metal and is called *verdigris*.

It would be a simple task to make a list of other similar substances, following our principle of likelihood. And if, for relaxation, one gives up discussing eternal things, it is reasonable and sensible to occupy one's leisure in a way that brings pleasure and no regrets, by considering likely accounts of the world of change. So let us now indulge ourselves and proceed with an account of the probabilities next in order.

1. Scion: 'shoot of plant, esp. one cut for grafting or planting; descendant', O.E.D. The chief characteristic of anything to which the Greeks applied the word 'adamant' was hardness. It is uncertain to what substance Plato is here referring.

29. (c) *Mixtures of water. Refrigeration and 'juices'.*

We begin with water that is mixed with fire, which is
fine and liquid (it owes its name 'liquid' to its motion and
the way it rolls over the ground),[1] and also yielding because
its bases are less stable than those of earth and give way.
This, when left free of fire and air and isolated, becomes more
uniform and is compressed by the particles leaving it and
solidified. When the process is complete, if it takes place
above the earth the result is hail, if on the earth ice; when it is
incomplete and the water only half-solidified, the result
above the earth is snow, while on earth the consequent
freezing of the dew is called hoar-frost.

Most of the varieties of water are mixtures, which we call
generally 'juices', because they are filtered through plants;
and because they are mixtures the number of different 60
combinations is large and most of them have no specific
name. But there are four named varieties which contain fire
and are specially conspicuous. (1) Wine, which warms body
and soul together. (2) An oily variety, which is smooth and
splits the visual ray and is consequently bright and gleaming
to the eye and shiny in appearance:[2] pitch, castor oil, olive
oil, and other substances with the same properties. (3) All
varieties which give a natural relaxation to the pores of the
mouth and so produce the sensation of sweetness, to which
the general name *honey* is given. (4) Lastly, what we call *acid*,
which burns and dissolves the flesh, a frothy substance quite
distinct from all other juices.

30. (d) *Varieties and mixtures of earth.*

Of the varieties of earth, that which has been strained
through water becomes story substance in the following
way. The water mixed with it is broken down in the process

1. There is a play upon words in the Greek.
2. Cf. pp. 94-5 below.

of mixture, becomes air, and thrusts up towards its own region. But the space above it is not empty, and accordingly it thrusts against the neighbouring air. Under the thrust the weight of this bears upon the mass of earth, compresses it violently, and drives it into the place left by the newly formed air. The earth so compressed by air becomes insoluble stone, the finer variety being transparent and composed of equal and uniform particles, the poorer varieties being the opposite.

When earth loses all its moisture quickly over a fast fire the product is more brittle being what we have generically named earthenware. But sometimes there is some moisture left and the product, when it cools, is fusible by fire, being lava.[1]

There are two other substances formed in the same way when water has been extracted in large quantity from a mixture; both are formed of finer particles, both taste salty, and both become only semi-solid and are soluble in water. The one, which cleanses from grease or dirt, is soda; the other, which blends well in various flavours, is salt, a substance traditionally acceptable to heaven.[2]

Some compounds of earth and water are soluble by fire but not by water, the reason being as follows: (1) Fire and air do not dissolve masses of earth, because their particles are smaller than the interstices in the earth's texture, and so they have plenty of room to pass through without exerting force and leave it unbroken and undissolved; but particles of water, being larger than the interstices, have to force their way through and so break down the earth and dissolve it. If earth has not been forcibly compressed, only water will dissolve it in this way; if it has been so compressed, only fire will dissolve it for nothing else can penetrate it. (2) Water again, when under extreme compression can be dispersed only by fire, but when under less compression, by both fire

61

1. Meaning uncertain: but a parallel with Aristotle (*Meteorologica*, 383b, 9) suggests that the meaning is 'lava'.
2. Reading κατὰ νόμον 60e, 1.

and air, air penetrating its interstices, fire also breaking it down into its triangles. (3) Air under forcible compression can be resolved only into its basic units, when not so compressed can be dissolved only by fire. Compounds of earth and water behave accordingly. So long as the interstices in the earth, reduced in size by compression though they be, are filled with water, particles of water from outside cannot penetrate them and so flow over them and leave them undissolved; but the particles of fire penetrate the interstices of the water and have the same effect on it as it has on earth, and are thus the sole agent that can cause these compounds to dissolve and melt. Some of them contain less water than earth, namely glass and fusible stones of all kinds; some have more water, namely substances with a consistency like wax and incense.

31. *The physical basis of sensation.*
    (*a*) *Tactile qualities: hot, cold; hard, soft; heavy, light; smooth, rough.*

We have now sufficiently illustrated the varieties of substance due to the shapes, combinations, and mutual transformations of the primary bodies. We must go on to explain how they come to have their sensible qualities. Our argument must presuppose the existence of sensation, though we have not yet described the formation of the body and its properties or of the mortal part of the soul. Yet it is impossible to give an adequate account of them without reference to sensible qualities and vice versa; and equally impossible to treat both together. We must therefore assume the existence of one or other and return later to examine what we have assumed. To enable us to proceed straight from the four kinds of body to their sensible qualities, let us therefore make the necessary assumptions about body and soul.

Let us first see why it is we call fire 'hot'. We can begin by calling to mind the dividing and cutting effect of it on our own bodies; for we all know that the sensation it gives is a piercing one. The fineness of its edges, the sharpness of its angles, the smallness of its particles and its speed of movement – all of which give it the force and penetration to cut 62 into anything it encounters – can be explained when we remember the formation of its figure; and we may conclude that its special ability to penetrate and disintegrate our bodies gives what we call 'heat' its quality and name.[1]

Its opposite is obvious enough, but we must not fail to explain it. When particles of liquids adjacent to the body enter it they drive out particles smaller than themselves and, being unable to make their way into the space thus left, compress the moisture in us, which instead of being without uniformity and mobile becomes immobile, uniform, and compressed, and so solidifies. But what is subjected to unnatural contraction naturally struggles to counteract it, and this struggling and shaking is called trembling and shivering, and the name 'cold' is given both to the sensation as a whole and to what produces it.

'Hard' is anything to which our flesh yields, 'soft' is anything which yields to our flesh; and we use the same terms generally of things which stand in this relation. Yielding substances have a small base; but substances which have square bases and so stand firmest retain their shape most stubbornly; so also those most highly compressed are most resistant.

'Heavy' and 'light' can be most easily explained in the context of an examination of the meaning of 'above' and 'below'. For it is quite wrong to suppose that the universe is divided by nature into two opposite regions, one 'below', to which sink all bodies with weight, and one 'above', to which no body rises of its own accord. For since the universe is spherical all points at extreme distance from the centre are equidistant from it, and so all equally 'extremes'; while the centre, being equidistant from the extremes is equally 'opposite' to them all. This being the structure of the

1. A play upon words in the Greek.

universe, it would be inappropriate to use the terms 'above'
and 'below' of any of the regions we have mentioned. For
it is not right to describe its central region as 'above' or
'below' but simply as the centre; and the circumference is
not, of course, at the centre, nor does any part of it differ
from any other by being closer to the centre than any part
opposite to it. Indeed, can contrary terms be properly
applied to any completely uniform object? For if there were
a solid in equipoise at the centre, it would never move
towards any of its extreme points because of their complete   63
uniformity; while if anyone moved round its circumference
he would repeatedly be standing at his own antipodes and
so refer to the same point as both above and below. So,
since as we have said the universe is spherical, there is no
sense in referring to any region of it as 'above' or 'below'.
The source of these terms and their proper application, by
transference from which we have got into the habit of
using them to describe the world as a whole, we may explain
on the following supposition. Imagine a man standing in the
region of the universe allotted to fire, to which fire tends to
move and in which is the greatest mass of it; suppose him to
be able to detach portions of fire and weigh them in the
scales of a balance, which he raises forcibly into the alien air.
Clearly it requires less force to raise the smaller portion
than the larger; for when two masses are lifted by the same
force the resistance of the larger to the lifting force must be
greater than that of the smaller; and the larger will be said
to be 'heavy' and to tend 'downwards', the smaller to be
'light' and to tend 'upwards'. This is precisely what we
ought to detect ourselves doing in our own region. When
we stand on the earth and try to weigh[1] earthy substances, or
sometimes pure earth, we lift them into the alien air by force
and against their natural tendency, as they cling to the
matter kindred to them. So the smaller mass yields more
readily than the larger to the force applied to it and rises into
the alien element; and we call it 'light' and the region into

1. More literally, 'distinguish between'.

which it is forced 'above', and use 'heavy' and 'below' in the opposite sense. These terms must thus be purely relative because the main aggregates of the basic kinds of matter occupy opposite regions to each other; and what is light or heavy or below or above in one region will be found to be or to become the direct opposite of what has these characteristics in another region or to be angularly inclined to it at different degrees. The general principle in all cases is that the tendency of any body to move towards its kindred aggregate makes it 'heavy', and that the region to which it moves is 'below', and vice versa.

So much for our explanation of these terms. The qualities smooth and rough are easy to understand and explain. The second is due to a combination of hardness and unevenness, 64 the first to a combination of evenness and density.

32. *Pleasure and pain.*

There remains one major problem to be dealt with in our discussion of the bodily sensations as a whole, and that is how the sensations we have so far described give rise to pleasurable and painful feelings, and further how various other processes which give rise to sensation in the parts of the body may in turn be accompanied by inherent pains and pleasures.

In any account of qualities sensible or non-sensible we must remember the distinction we have already made between substances of a mobile and of an immobile structure; this is the clue which our investigations should follow. For what is naturally mobile, when affected by even a slight impulse, spreads it round, one particle passing it on to another until it reaches the consciousness and reports the quality of the agent. By contrast, what is immobile is too stable to spread or communicate to its neighbours the effect of any modification it suffers, and so, as the particles do not pass it on to each other, the original modification does not affect the creature as a whole, which remains unconscious of it. This is what happens with bone and hair and the other parts of our body which are composed mostly of earth; the reverse is true of sight and hearing in particular, as they have in them the highest proportion of the qualities of fire and air. Pleasure and pain, then, we must think of as follows. Any sudden and violent disturbance of our normal state is painful, and a sudden return to it pleasurable; small and gentle disturbances are imperceptible, their opposites perceptible. Processes which take place with ease are in the highest degree perceptible, but cause neither pain nor pleasure, for example visual perception which we described earlier[1] as a physical body formed in daylight in extension of ourselves. No pain is caused by cuts and burns and other modifications to which this is subject, and no pleasure by its return to normal, though from its modifications and its contact with objects on which it impinges we receive our clearest and most important perceptions; for no violence is involved when it is broken or reformed. But organs composed of larger particles, which resist action upon them and transmit its effects generally, are subject to pleasures and pains, pains when their balance is upset, pleasure when it is 65 restored. And bodies subject to wastage and depletion which is gradual, but to sudden large-scale replenishment, are unconscious of the depletion but conscious of the replenishment, and the mortal part of their soul experiences no pain but intense pleasure – pleasant smells are a good example. But when the balance is upset suddenly and restored gradually and with difficulty the results are the opposite; of this burns and cuts are a good example.

33. (b) Tastes.

That pretty well covers sensations common to the body as a whole and the names given to the agents that cause them.

1. p. 62.

We must now see if we can account for sensations that occur in particular organs and for their causative agents. We must first explain what we left out in our account of 'juices', that is, the various sensations peculiar to the tongue. Like most others they are due to contraction and relaxation, but depend more than others on roughness and smoothness. So (1) when particles of earth enter the discriminatory passages which extend from tongue to heart, melt on contact with the moist and soft flesh and contract and dry the vessels, they produce, if comparatively rough, a sour taste, if less rough, a dry taste. (2) Substances which rinse these vessels and generally act as detergents to the tongue, if their action is excessive to the point of dissolving the substance of the tongue, like soda, are all called bitter; but if their action is less violent than that of soda and the rinsing effect is moderate, they taste salty, and are agreeable to us without any jarring bitter effect. (3) Things which absorb warmth from the mouth and are softened by it, become hot and in turn

66 burn what heated them, and rising because of their lightness to the sense organs in the head, cut everything on which they impinge, and, because they have this effect, are called 'pungent'. (4) Again there are particles[1] of substances broken down by decomposition which make their way into the narrow passages; these particles are duly proportioned to the earthy and airy particles contained there, which they stir into motion, causing them to surround each other, one kind of particle finding its way into hollows formed by the other and stretching round it. So hollow films of moisture, either pure or with an admixture of earth, are formed, and produce liquid air-containers or hollow spheres of water; these if pure and transparent are called bubbles, if mixed with earth and rising in a mass are spoken of as boiling and fermentation. And what is responsible for these effects is called 'acid'. (5) An effect opposite to all those thus described is produced by an opposite cause. When the composition of the substances entering the mouth in liquid form is

1. Reading τὰ γὲ αὖ 66a, 2.

akin to the structure of the tongue, they smooth and mollify its roughened parts, and contract or relax, as the case may be, any unnatural relaxation or contraction, restoring its natural state; and any such remedy for states externally imposed is pleasant and agreeable and has been given the name 'sweet'.

34. (c) Smells.

So much for tastes. Our faculty of smell has no definite pattern. All smells are half-formed things, and none of our regular figures corresponds to any particular smell. The passages of smell are too narrow for earth and water, and too wide for fire and air, so none of them is perceptible to smell; smells occur when substances are in process of liquefaction, decomposition, dissolution, or evaporation. They arise in the intermediate stage of the transformation of water into air or air into water, and are to be classed as vapour when it is from water to air. So all are rarer than water but denser than air. This can be seen when one breathes air in forcibly through something that obstructs the passage of the breath; no smell percolates through, but the air comes through devoid of any smell. These are therefore two groups into 67 which the diversities of smell fall. They have no names and do not consist of a plurality of definite types; the only clear distinction we can make is between the pleasant and unpleasant. The unpleasant roughens and does violence to the whole cavity between crown and navel; the pleasant soothes it and restores it agreeably to its natural condition.

35. (d) Sounds.

The third organ of sense which we must examine is hearing, and we must explain the various sensations occurring in it. Sound may be generally defined as an impulse given by the air through the ears to the brain and blood and passed on to the soul; and the consequent motion which starts from the head and terminates in the region of the liver is hearing. Rapid movement produces high-pitched sound, and the slower the motion the lower the pitch. Regular motion gives a uniform, smooth sound, irregular motion a harsh sound. Large and small motions produce loud and soft sounds. Relationships between sounds we must deal with later.[1]

36. (e) Colours.

There remains a fourth type of sensation which has a large number of diversities that need classification, diversities to which we give the general name colour, which is a kind of flame that streams off bodies of various kinds and is composed of particles so proportioned to our sight as to yield sensation. The bare facts about the causes of vision we have already mentioned. The following is a reasonably likely account of particular colours.

The particles which impinge on the visual ray from other bodies are either larger or smaller than those of the visual ray itself or else the same size. If they are the same size they are imperceptible or as we say 'transparent'. If they are larger they compress the ray, if they are smaller they penetrate it; here there is an analogy with what is hot or cold to the touch and what is astringent or burning ('pungent' as we call it) to the tongue, the same effects being produced in a different medium, and appearing for the reasons given with a corresponding difference as 'black' and 'white'. We must assign these names accordingly, calling that which penetrates the visual ray 'white' and that which compresses it 'black'.

When another kind of fire with a faster motion falls on the visual ray and penetrates it right up to the eyes it forces apart and dissolves the passages in the eyes, and causes the dis-

1. p. 109.

charge of a mass of fire and water which we call a tear; this **68**
incoming fire meets a fire moving towards it, and the outgoing fire leaps out like lightning while the incoming is
quenched in the moisture. The result is a confusion of all
kinds of colours; this we call 'dazzling' and the object which
produces it 'bright' and 'gleaming'.

Then there is a variety of fire intermediate between these
which reaches the moisture of the eye and mixes with it, but
is not 'gleaming'; the radiance of this fire shining through
the moisture with which it is mingled produces a blood-like
colour which is called 'red'.

Bright mixed with red and white produces orange. There
would be no sense in giving the proportions, even if one
knew them; for one could not be even moderately sure of
giving either necessary proof or reasonable estimate.[1]

Red mixed with black and white gives purple, or deep
blue when these ingredients are well burnt and more black
added. Tawny-yellow is a mixture of orange and grey, grey
being a mixture of black and white, while pale yellow is a
mixture of orange and white. White combined with bright
and immersed in deep black produces blue-black, which in
turn produces blue-green when mixed with white, while
tawny-yellow and black yield green.

These examples make it pretty clear by what mixtures we
should represent other colours if we are to preserve our
principle of giving a likely account. But to try to apply an
experimental test would be to show ignorance of the difference between human nature and divine; for god has the
knowledge and the power that makes him able to blend
many constituents into one and to resolve the resulting
unity again into its constituents, but no man can or will ever
be able to do either.

1. There is a transition here from the blending of light to the mixing
of pigments. Greek colour-words are sometimes hard to identify; the
Greeks seem to have looked at the colour-spectrum in a way different
from ours. Aristotle deals with the colours of the rainbow in *Meteorologica* III 4, 37b, 7 ff.

Main Section III. Reason and necessity working together.

37. *In the preceding section we have been concerned with the
necessary material constituents of the universe and the physical
processes which go on in them. These processes are subordinate
to the ultimate divine purpose, which makes the best out of
them that it can. In the remainder of our account we shall be
largely concerned with human physiology, where divine purpose
is again the important factor.*

*The subordinate gods take over from the Demiurge the divine
principle of soul (cf. p. 58), encase it in the globe of the skull,
and add the mortal parts of the soul to it.*

All these things were so constituted of necessity and the
maker of what is fairest and best in the realm of change took
them over when he produced the self-sufficient and perfect
god, using this type of cause as subordinate but himself
contriving the good in things that come to be. We must
therefore distinguish two types of cause, the necessary and
the divine. The divine we should look for in all things for
the sake of the measure of happiness in life that our nature
permits, and the necessary for the sake of the divine, reflecting that without them we cannot perceive, apprehend,
or in any way attain our objective. Now, therefore, that the
two kinds of cause which we need as material for the fabric
of the rest of our account have been sifted out, let us briefly
return to our starting point and retrace the steps that led us
to the point which we have now once more reached, and
then attempt to bring our story to a final conclusion.

As we said at the beginning, these things were in disorder
till god introduced measurable relations, internal and external, among them, to the degree and extent that they were
capable of proportion and measurement. For at first they
stood in no such relations, except by chance, nor was there
anything that deserved the names – fire, water, and the rest –
which we now use. But he reduced them to order, and then
put together this universe out of them, a single living

creature containing in itself all other living things mortal and immortal. He made the divine with his own hands, but he ordered his own children to make the generation of mortals. They took over from him an immortal principle of soul, and, imitating him, encased it in a mortal physical globe, with the body as a whole for vehicle. And they built on to it another mortal part, containing terrible and necessary feelings: pleasure, the chief incitement to wrong, pain, which frightens us from good, confidence and fear, two foolish counsellors, obstinate passion and credulous hope. To this mixture they added irrational sensation and desire which shrinks from nothing, and so gave the mortal element its indispensable equipment.

38. *The mortal parts of the soul. Plato assumes the threefold division of the soul into reason (here called divine), emotion and appetite (both here called mortal) which he had made in the* Republic. *The emotions are located in the region of the heart, the appetites in the belly. The function of various organs described: heart and lung, liver and spleen, intestines.*

And since they shrank from polluting the divine element with these mortal feelings more than was absolutely necessary, they located the mortal element in a separate part of the body, and constructed the neck as a kind of isthmus and boundary between head and breast to keep them apart. The mortal element they secured in the breast and trunk (as we call it); and since it has a better and a worse part, they divided the hollow of the trunk by inserting the midriff as a partition, rather as a house is divided into men and women's quarters.

The part of the soul which is the seat of courage, passion and ambition they located nearer the head between midriff and neck; there it would be well-placed to listen to the commands of reason and combine with it in forcibly restraining the appetites when they refused to obey the word of

70

command from the citadel. They stationed the heart, which links the veins and is the source of the blood which circulates through the body's members, in the guardroom, in order that when passion was roused to boiling point by news of wrong being done, whether by external action or internally by the appetites, commands and threats should circulate quickly through the body's narrow ways, and any sentient part of it listen obediently and submit to the control of the best. And because they knew that the swelling of the heart which makes it throb with suspense or anger was due to fire, they devised relief for it in the structure of the lung, which they made soft and bloodless, full of cavities like a sponge, and so able, by absorbing breath and drink, to provide relief and ease from the heat. For this reason they cut the channels of the windpipe to the lung and set it round the heart like a cushion, so that when passion was at its height, the heart would beat against something yielding, be refreshed, and so because less distressed better able to assist courage in the service of reason.

The appetite for food and drink and other natural needs of the body they located between the midriff and the region of the navel, building in the area a kind of manger for the body's food; and they secured appetite there like a wild beast, which must be fed with the rest of us if mortals were to exist at all. And they put it in this position in order that it might continue to feed at its stall, but be as far as possible from the seat of deliberation, and cause the least possible noise and disturbance, so leaving the highest part of us to deliberate quietly about the welfare of each and all. And knowing that it would not understand reason or be capable of paying attention to rational argument even if it became aware of it, but would easily fall under the spell of images and phantoms by day or night, god played upon this weakness and formed the liver, which he put into the creature's stall. He made it smooth and close in texture, sweet and bitter, so that the influence of the mind could project thoughts upon it which it would receive and reflect in the

71

form of visible images, like a mirror. When the mind wants to cause fear, it makes use of the liver's native bitterness and plays a stern and threatening role, quickly infusing the whole organ with bitterness and giving it a bilious colour; at the same time it contracts the liver and makes it all wrinkled and rough, bending and shrivelling the lobe, blocking and closing the vessels leading to it and so causing pain and nausea. By contrast, gentle thoughts from the mind produce images of the opposite kind, which will neither produce nor have connection with anything of a contrary nature to their own, and so bring relief from bitterness, using the organ's innate sweetness to render it straight and smooth and free, and making the part of the soul that lives in the region of the liver cheerful and gentle, and able to spend the night quietly in divination and dreams, as reason and understanding are beyond it. For our makers remembered that their father had ordered them to make mortal creatures as perfect as possible, and so did their best even with this base part of us and gave it the power of prophecy so that it might have some apprehension of truth. And clear enough evidence that god gave this power to man's irrational part is to be found in our incapacity for inspired and true prophecy when in our right minds; we only achieve it when the power of our understanding is inhibited in sleep, or when we are in an abnormal condition owing to disease or divine inspiration. And it is the function of someone in his right mind to construe what is remembered of utterances made in dream or waking by those who have the gift of prophecy and divine inspiration, and to give a rational interpretation of their visions, saying what good or evil they portend and for 72 whom, whether future, past, or present. It is not the business of any man, so long as he is in an abnormal state, to interpret his own visions and utterances; there is truth in the old saying that only a sane man can attend to his own concerns and know himself. Hence the custom of setting up spokesmen to pronounce judgement on inspired prophecies; they are sometimes called prophets by those who are ignorant that they are in fact not prophets, but expounders of riddling oracles and visions, and so most exactly called spokesmen of those who prophesy.

Such then, is the nature and position of the liver, which enables it to carry out its function of prophecy. So long as any creature is alive, the liver gives comparatively clear indications, but after death it becomes blind and its signs too obscure to convey any clear meaning. The structure and position of the organ immediately on its left enable it to keep the liver bright and clean, like a duster kept handy to clean a mirror. For the spleen, whose texture is hollow and bloodless, absorbs and clears away any impurities which occur in the region of the liver because of diseases in the body. When filled with these impurities it becomes swollen and infected, but when the body is purged it subsides and resumes its original state.

That concludes our account of the mortal and divine parts of the soul, where they are placed and with what organs and why. Only divine confirmation would justify us in asserting its truth; but we may venture to claim now, and still more on further reflection, that it is likely, so let us do so. Our next topic must be pursued on the same principles; it is the way in which the rest of the body came to be. Its constitution can best be viewed with the following considerations in mind. Those who framed our species knew how ungovernable our appetite for drink and food would be, and how we should out of sheer greed consume more than a moderate or 73 necessary amount; in order therefore to prevent our rapid destruction by disease and the prompt and untimely disappearance of our species, they made the lower belly, as it is called, into a receptacle to contain superfluous food and drink, and wound the bowels round in coils, thus preventing the quick passage of food, which would otherwise compel the body to want more and make its appetite insatiable, so rendering our species incapable through gluttony of philosophy and culture, and unwilling to listen to the divinest element in us.

39. *The main structure of the human frame.*
The marrow (regarded as life-substance and seed).

Bone, flesh, and the other tissues were constituted as follows. Their starting point was the formation of the marrow; and the bonds of life, which tie soul and body together and are the roots of the mortal creature, were made fast in the marrow which was itself formed of other materials. From each particular type of triangle the god set aside those that were smooth and unwarped and so able to produce the purest fire, water, air and earth; these he mixed in due proportion to produce marrow, as a kind of universal seed for mortal creatures of every kind. In it he firmly implanted the different kinds of soul, dividing the marrow in his initial distribution into as many different varieties and the particular forms as it was destined to bear. And he moulded into spherical shape the part of the marrow (the ploughland, as it were) that was to contain the divine seed and called it the brain, indicating that when each creature was completed the vessel containing the brain should be the head.[1] The rest of the marrow that was to contain the mortal parts of the soul he divided into long, cylindrical sections, called by the general name 'marrow', to which the whole soul was anchored. And round brain and marrow, for which he first constructed a bony protective covering, he went on to frame our whole body.

40. *Bone, sinews, and flesh; distribution of flesh on the frame;*
skin, hair, and nails.

He put bone together as follows. He sifted out earth that was pure and smooth, kneaded it and steeped it in marrow; next he placed it in fire and then again into water, then back into fire and then again into water, and by this repetition of the process rendered it insoluble by either. From the result-

1. In Greek the words for 'brain' and 'head' are similar.

74 ant substance he formed a spherical bony sphere to contain
the brain, having only a narrow outlet: and to surround the
marrow in neck and back he moulded vertebrae from it and
balanced them like pivots through the whole span of the
trunk, starting from the head. The seed was thus entirely
fenced in and protected by a bony container, jointed to
provide for movement and flexibility, in whose construction
the property of Difference kept the parts distinct. But he
thought that the constitution of bone was unduly brittle and
inflexible, and that when subjected in turn to heat and cold
it would mortify and destroy the seed within it, and for that
reason devised the sinews and flesh. The sinews bind all the
limbs together, and by contracting and relaxing enable the
body to bend and stretch about its joints. The flesh was to
serve as a protection against heat and a shelter against cold,
besides being a kind of padded garment to cushion us softly
and gently against falls; it also contained warm moisture
and so was able to provide a cooling system of its own in
summer by sweating out this moisture over the whole body,
and a reasonable protection against the assaults of the en-
veloping frost in winter by its internal warmth. With this in
mind he who modelled us composed our flesh, soft and full of
sap, by making a suitably proportioned compound of water,
fire and earth, and adding a ferment of acid and salt to the
mixture; the sinews he made from an unfermented mixture of
bone and flesh, producing a substance intermediate between
the two and adding a yellow colour. The sinews are thus
tenser and tougher than flesh, but softer and more elastic
than bone. The two of them the god wrapped round bones
and marrow, tying the bones together with sinews, and
making a shelter for them with flesh. The bones which were
most alive[1] he gave the thinnest covering of flesh, and those
least alive the thickest and most plentiful; and he caused
little flesh to grow at the joints of the bones, except where
reason required it. His purpose was, firstly, to avoid making
the body clumsy and immobile by hindering the movement

1. i.e. contained most of the life-substance, marrow.

of the joints, and, secondly, to avoid making it insensitive because of the thickness of many superimposed layers of flesh, so hampering memory and receptiveness of mind. So thigh and shin, hips, upper and lower arm, and other 75 bones within the body that are unjointed or devoid of intelligence, because they contain little soul in their marrow, are well covered with flesh; but parts where there is intelligence are, in general, less well covered, though there are exceptions like the tongue where the flesh is itself formed for the purpose of sensation. For it is one of the limitations of the human frame with which we are necessarily born and which grows with us that thickness of bone and abundance of flesh cannot be combined with quickness of perception. For if these two characteristics were able to coincide they would certainly have done so in the structure of the head, and with a head fortified with flesh and sinew human life would have been twice or many times as long as at present, as well as healthier and more free from pain. As it was, those who produced our species had to work out whether to produce a longer-lived but inferior type or a shorter-lived but superior, and decided that a shorter and better life was in all respects preferable to a longer but poorer one. So they covered the head with thin bone, but not with flesh or sinews, because it had no joints; which is why the head attached to man's body combines a large degree of perceptiveness and intelligence with a much smaller degree of structural strength. On the same principles and in the same way the god fastened sinews uniformly in a ring round the neck at the base of the head, and tied the end of the jaw bones to them just under the face; the remainder he distributed among the various limbs to hold the joints together. The mouth was given by our makers its present equipment of teeth, tongue, and lips because this was both necessary and for our good; what enters the mouth is necessary, in the sense that the food it takes in is necessary to nourish the body, what goes out of it is good in the sense that the outgoing stream of speech is the servant of intelligence and so the highest and best of all streams. They were also unable to leave the bone of the skull bare because of the extremes of seasonal heat and cold, but could not let it become dull and insensitive under a heavy shelter of flesh. So without drying up entirely, the flesh formed a loosely-fitting film which we now call skin; this film closed in on itself and grew round over the head to cover it owing to the action of the moisture in the brain, which made its way up through the sutures, damped the skin and made it close up into a kind of knot on the crown. (The sutures are of very different patterns owing to the varied action of the circles and the nourishing material, being greater or fewer in number according to the intensity of the struggle[1] between the two.) This covering of skin was pricked all over by the fire of the divine part,[2] and the moisture made its way out through the perforations. Such of it as was pure liquid and heat escaped, but that mixed with the ingredients from which the skin was made was driven outwards and stretched into a long external thread whose fineness was equal to the size of the puncture; but the pressure of the surrounding air slowed up its motion and made it coil up under the skin and take root there. This is the process that caused hair to grow on the skin; it is a fibrous substance of the same nature as skin, but harder and denser because of the felting process caused by refrigeration, a process which operates on each hair as it emerges from the skin. Our maker thus gave us shaggy heads, using the physical means we have just described, but with the intention of providing an alternative form of shelter to flesh to shield the brain; for hair is light, and provides adequate shade in summer and protection in winter without hindering quickness of perception. And where fingers and toes were finally knitted up, a mixture of sinew, skin, and bone combined to form, when dried out, a single hard covering. These were the physical means used to make it, but its

1. Cf. p. 60.
2. i.e. the brain; the marrow composing the brain appears to contain fire (p. 101).

governing purpose looked to future creations. For those who framed us knew that later on women and other animals would be produced from men, and that many creatures would need claws and hoofs for different purposes; so they provided the rudiments of them in men at their first creation, and for this reason and by these means caused skin, hair and nails to grow at the extremities of the limbs.

41. *Plants.*

The parts and limbs of the mortal creature were thus brought together into a whole which must of necessity live its life exposed to fire and air, be worn away and wasted by them, and finally perish. And to support it the gods devised and brought into being a substance akin to it, but with different form and senses, another kind of living thing, trees, plants and seeds. These we have today schooled and domesticated to our purposes by agriculture, but at first there were only the wild varieties, which are the older of the two. Everything that has life has every right to be called a living thing; and the group of which we are speaking has the third sort of soul, which we have located between midriff and navel, and which is without belief or reason or understanding but has appetite and a sense of pleasure and pain. It is always entirely passive; its formation has not allowed it to perceive and reflect on its own nature,[1] by revolving in and about itself, rejecting motion from without and exercising a motion of its own. So it is a creature with a life of its own, but it cannot move and is fixed and rooted because it has no self-motion.

77

1. Reading φύσιν.

42. *Digestion and respiration. In reading this section it must be remembered that there was very little knowledge of human anatomy in Plato's day; and the reader is well advised to follow Cornford's advice, forget anything he knows about human anatomy, and in that state of ignorance try to follow Plato's description step by step. There are two main elements in it: (a) the analogy of the fish-trap (b) the theory of circular thrust.*

When the higher powers had thus produced plants for us inferior creatures to feed on, they cut in our body a system of conduits, like water channels in a garden, to irrigate it with incoming moisture. First beneath the covering of skin and flesh they cut two veins along the back, like two water pipes, corresponding to the two sides of the body, right and left; these veins ran down beside the spine, to give vigour to the life-giving marrow which lay between them and to facilitate by their downward flow the even distribution of moisture to the rest of the body. Next they cut the veins in the head and wove them through one another in opposite directions, left to right and right to left, to help the skin in binding the head to the body as there were no sinews[1] holding it round the crown, and to ensure that sensations from either side should be conveyed to the whole body.

42. (a) *The fish-trap.*

They went on to contrive their irrigation system in a way that we shall best understand if we first agree on the following principle. All bodies composed of smaller particles are impervious to larger ones, but those composed of larger ones are not impervious to smaller; fire is composed of the smallest particles, and consequently penetrates water, earth and air and any bodies composed of them, which cannot remain impervious to it. The same principle must be applied

1. Cf. p. 103.

to the belly, which retains the solids and liquids it receives, but cannot retain air and fire whose particles are smaller than those of its own structure. The god availed himself of this in arranging the irrigation of the veins from the belly. He wove a network of air and fire, like a fish-trap, with two

FIGURE 6   FIGURE 7

The fish-trap. The fish-trap described is constructed on the principle used in the common lobster-pot. But the narrow entrance is contrived by inserting a separate funnel into the main body of the trap: Fig. 6. The trap is then transferred to the human body as illustrated in Fig. 7. The funnel, internally, leads to lungs and belly, and has a double exit, through mouth and nose, the exit through the nose being again subdivided.

funnels at its entrance, one of which was again double; from the funnels a network of reeds (as it were) extended right round to the far end of the structure. The interior of the network he made of fire, the funnels and the main framework of air. This structure he took and set it round the living creature he had formed. He inserted the two funnels into the mouth, and extended one of them downwards into the lung by way of the windpipes, and the other alongside the windpipes into the belly. The first channel he split again and brought the two subdivisions out together by way of the nostrils, so that when the other channel by way of the mouth was not working, there would be an alternative source of supply. The main part of the fish-trap he attached round the hollow of our body, and gave the whole an alternating movement, a flow into the funnels (gentle, as they are made of air) being followed by a flow back, while the network correspondingly sinks in or out through the body, which is porous, and the attached rays of the internal fire follow the movement of air in either direction.[1] This movement continues so long as the mortal creature survives, and is the process to which we say the names inhalation and exhalation have been given. This whole action and reaction results in our body being fed and kept alive by moisture and refrigeration. For the internal fire follows the air in its movement (being structurally connected with it) and, as it surges in and out, enters the belly and takes hold of the food and drink there, breaks it up small and disintegrates it, and carries it through the channels along which it passes, discharging it into the veins like water from a spring into conduits and making the currents in the veins flow through the body as if through an aqueduct.

42. (b) *Circular thrust. The basis of the theory is that in a world in which there is no void, movement can only take place by a process of mutual replacement of one substance by another. But the Greeks had no idea of momentum, believing that all motion required the continuous exercise of force, and the theory was also used (by Aristotle as well as by Plato) to account for the motion of projectiles, as well as for other processes listed here.*

   1. The material of the 'network' is fire and air which can pass in and out through the pores of the flesh, which is made of coarser material. And in some way not easy to visualize in detail the inner parts of the network are made of fire, the outer parts of air.

But we must look again at the process of respiration and
see what causes it to take place as it does. Since there is no
void into which a moving body can move, but the breath
does move out of our body, it follows clearly that it does
not move into a void but displaces the adjacent air. This
process of displacement is continuous, and so of necessity
the air is thrust round into the space originally vacated by
the breath; this it enters and refills, replacing the breath. The
whole process is continuous and circular and due to there
being no void. So the chest and lungs when they expel the
breath are filled again by the air surrounding the body, which
is driven in through the porous flesh by the circular thrust;
and when the flow of air is reversed and moves out through
the body it in turn thrusts the breath round and in through
mouth and nostrils. The original cause of these processes
is as follows. In every creature the blood and veins are the
hottest part, constituting a kind of internal source of fire. So
in our simile of the fish-trap we said that all the inner parts
were woven of fire, the external of air. Heat, we must agree,
moves out to its like in its own region. And as there are two
outlets, one through the body, the other through mouth and
nostrils, when heat moves in one direction it gives a thrust
in the other; and the air so thrust falls into fire and is heated,
while the air which moves out is cooled. And as the air
which enters by either outlet rises in temperature, it recoils
because of its greater heat and moves towards its like, thrust-
ing air round to the other passage. This air again is similarly
affected and reacts in the same way, and the two impulses set
up a continuous cycle of action and reaction which produces
our inhalation and exhalation.

The action of cupping glasses, the process of swallowing,
and the behaviour of projectiles discharged either into the   80
air or along the ground, are to be explained on the same
principle; so also are sounds which seem high or low according to their speed of travel and concordant or dissonant
according to the correspondence or lack of correspondence
in the motions they set up in us. The slower sounds when

they catch up with the motions of the faster sounds which arrived earlier find these dying away and already corresponding to the motions which they themselves impart on their arrival; when they do arrive they do not cause discord by introducing a fresh motion, but produce an experience in which high and low are blended, because the slow motion now beginning corresponds with the faster one just coming to an end. So they give a thrill to fools and true enjoyment to the wise by reproducing divine melody in mortal movements. Other examples are any stream of flowing water, the fall of thunderbolts, and the puzzling attraction of amber and lodestone. In fact there is no 'attraction'. Proper investigation shows that there is no void and that circular thrust operates in all these instances; the various bodies part or come together in the course of mutual interchanges of position and what seems like magic is due to the complication of their effects on each other.

It is in this way and by these means, as we said before, that the process of respiration takes place, from which this digression started. Fire cuts up our food, and as it ebbs and flows within the body with the motion of the breath, its ebb and flow fill the veins with the cut-up food which it pumps into them from the belly. And this process keeps the streams of nourishment flowing through the body of all animals. The mixture of particles newly cut from kindred substances – fruit and vegetables which god caused to grow to provide food for us – contains all sorts of colours but is mainly pervaded by a red hue, the result of the operation of fire which stains it as it cuts it up. This is how the blood, as we call it, which runs in our body, gets the colour we have described; it feeds the flesh and the whole body, whose parts draw on it to replenish their loss by depletion. Replacement and wastage take place on the universal principle by which like always moves to like. For the elements around us are constantly breaking down the human body and distributing each type of constituent to its like; so analogously the constituents of the blood, broken up small and surrounded by the living organism as by a containing heaven, must of necessity move to the universal rhythm, each fragment moving to its like and replenishing previous wastage.

43. *Normal growth and decay; natural death.*

Decline is caused by excess of wastage over intake, growth by the opposite. And when the structure of the creature is new, and the triangles of its constituent elements fresh from the workshop, as it were, they are locked firmly together, though the consistency of the whole aggregate is soft, having been recently formed of marrow and fed on milk. So the triangles composing the food and drink which it takes into itself from outside are older and weaker than those in itself, which are new and break them up and absorb them, feeding the creature on substances like its own and making it grow. But when the root of the triangles is loosened by the many trials they meet in the course of time, they can no longer cut up into their own likeness the triangles of the food taken in, but are themselves easily broken up by the newcomers; and in the process the creature fails and declines into the condition which we call old age. Finally, when the bonds of the triangles in the marrow fail and part under the stress, the bonds of the soul are also loosened; and when this happens in the course of nature the soul departs gladly – for everything that takes place naturally is pleasant, whereas what is contrary to nature is painful. So a death by disease or injury is painful and unwelcome, but one that brings life to its natural close by old age is of all deaths least distressing and brings more pleasure than pain.

44. *Diseases of the body. (a) Due to lack of balance between the four elements.*

The origin of diseases should be obvious. The body is   82

composed of four elements – earth, fire, air and water; and disorders and diseases are caused by an unnatural excess or deficiency of any of them, by their shifting from their proper place to another, by any part of the body taking in an unsuitable variety either of fire or another element (for there are several varieties of them), and by similar disturbances. For if there is any unnatural formation or change of place in the elements, parts that were cool become heated, the dry becomes moist, what was light becomes heavy, and every kind of change takes place. The only way, in fact, in which good health can be maintained is for replacement and waste to be uniform, similar and on the same scale; any trespass beyond these limits in the process will give rise to all kinds of change, and to endless disease and deteriorations.

44. (*b*) *Diseases of the 'secondary formations' – marrow, bone, flesh, sinew, blood.*

And as there are secondary formations in nature, it is possible to discern a second category of diseases. Marrow and bone and flesh and sinew, and, in a different way, blood, are all composed of the elements and though most diseases affecting them are caused in the way just described, the worst disorders are due to deterioration caused by reversal in the process of their formation. In the ordinary course of nature, flesh and sinew are formed from blood, sinew from the fibrine to which it is akin, flesh from the coagulation of what is left when the fibrine is removed. From sinews and flesh again proceeds a viscous oily fluid which glues the flesh to the bones as well as feeding the growth of the bone round the marrow; finally the purest part, consisting of the smoothest and most flexible triangles, filters through the thickness of the bone from which it distils in drops and waters the marrow. When the process takes place in this order the normal result is health, when the order is reversed it is disease. When flesh decomposes and the result of the decomposition is discharged back into the veins, the blood in the veins is extensively mixed with air and takes on a variety of colours and bitternesses, as well as acid and salty qualities, and develops bile, serum, and phlegm of all sorts. These undesirable and corrupt products first destroy the blood itself, and as they circulate through the veins provide no nourishment for the body and no longer maintain the natural orderly sequences; they conflict with each other 83 because of their mutual antipathy, they attack any constituent of the body that stands firm and sticks to its post, and spread destruction and decay. When the decomposing flesh is of old formation, it resists concoction and turns black under long exposure to high temperature; it is eaten right through, turns bitter in consequence, and becomes an attacking agent dangerous to any part of the body as yet uncorrupted. Sometimes it remains black but acquires acidity, losing its bitterness which is largely refined away; sometimes it retains its bitterness but an infusion of blood gives it a reddish tinge which combines with the black to produce a bilious colour;[1] finally, when the flesh decomposed by the inflammation is of new formation, yellow colour and bitterness are combined. The common name of all these products is bile, a name given either by doctors, or by someone capable of looking at a variety of phenomena and seeing a generic similarity which calls for a single name; the sub-species commonly recognized are each identified according to its particular colour.

As to serum, that of the blood is a mild lymph, but that of black and acid bile, when heat gives the mixture a saline quality, is a dangerous substance known as acid phlegm. There is a further substance that results from the decomposition of young and tender flesh in combination with air. This substance is inflated by air and enveloped by moisture to form bubbles which are individually too small to be seen, but visible in the mass, when they form froth, which looks

1. Reading χολῶδες 83b, 6.

white. The result of this decompositon of tender flesh in combination with air we call white phlegm. Phlegm newly formed produces lymph in the shape of sweat and tears and similar liquids daily excreted.

All these substances, then, are instrumental in producing disease, when the blood, instead of being replenished by food and drink in the natural way, draws its increase from the opposite source contrary to the ordinary course of nature.

When the various kinds of flesh are broken down by disease, but their foundations remain firm, the damage is 84 only half done, for recovery is easy. But when the fluid[1] that binds flesh and bone together is diseased and no longer separates from flesh and sinew to feed the bone and bind the flesh to it, but degenerates owing to an unhealthy way of life from its proper oily, smooth, viscous state into a rough, saline, parched condition, then the whole affected substance breaks away from the bones and crumbles into flesh and sinew, and the flesh, falling away from its roots leaves the sinews bare and full of brine, and falls back into the blood-stream where it aggravates the disorders already described.

Grievous as these afflictions of the body are, it is still worse when the cause of the trouble is more deep-seated. For example, thickness of the flesh may not allow the bone to breathe adequately. The consequent overheating causes the bone to decay, mortification sets in and it cannot absorb the fluid which feeds it; by a contrary process bone then dissolves back into fluid, fluid into flesh, flesh into blood, and the type of disorder produced is still more virulent than those already mentioned. But the worst case of all is when the marrow itself becomes diseased because of some deficiency or excess; the whole of the normal functioning of the body is then reversed and the most serious and fatal diseases result.

1. Reading νᾶμα in 84a, 2; but the reading and sense are uncertain. We have been told above (p. 112) that this fluid is produced from 'sinews and flesh', and I have translated accordingly, ignoring ἰνῶν.

44. (c) Diseases caused by breath, phlegm, and bile.

Next we must consider a third class of diseases which may
be subdivided into those caused (1) by breath, (2) by phlegm,
(3) by bile.

(1) When the lung, which provides the body with breath,
is blocked by rheums and its passages choked, the breath
does not reach some parts of the body, which putrify from
lack of air; other parts have too great a supply of air which
forces its way through the veins and contorts them, dissolves the body and is intercepted by the central barrier of
the diaphragm. This causes a large number of painful disorders, often accompanied by copious sweating. And when
the flesh disintegrates air is formed in the body and being
unable to escape causes the same acute pain as if it had been
introduced from outside, particularly when it gathers round
the sinews and connected veins and swells up, pulling back
the tendons and sinews attached to them. From the tension
so produced the consequent disorders are called tetanus and
opsithotonus. Their cure is difficult; they are generally
resolved by supervening fever.

(2) White phlegm if trapped in the body is dangerous
because of the air in the bubbles; it is less serious if it finds an
outlet, though it disfigures the surface of the body by producing white patches and similar complaints. Mixed with
black bile it can overlay and confuse the divine circles in the
head; if this happens in sleep the effect is comparatively mild,
but an attack in waking hours is more difficult to throw off.
And as the sacred part is affected, the disease is appropriately
called 'sacred'.[1] Acid, saline phlegm is the cause of all
disorders involving a discharge; these have a variety of
names corresponding to the variety of parts affected.

(3) All kinds of inflammation (so called from the burning
and heat which characterizes them) are caused by bile. If the
bile finds an outlet it produces various external eruptions;
if it is trapped inside, it produces many types of fever. The

1. Epilepsy.

worst is when it mixes with pure blood and causes disorder in the fibrine. The fibrine is distributed through the blood to secure a proper consistency and prevent it becoming so liquid owing to heat that it would run away through the porous texture of the body or so thick that it would be too sluggish to circulate in the veins. The normal composition of the fibrine preserves the right balance. And indeed if the fibrine from the blood of a corpse already cold is collected, the remaining blood runs out; but if it is left it soon congeals the blood with the assistance of the surrounding cold. This being the action of fibrine on blood, bile which was originally blood and now dissolves back into blood from flesh, on its first entry into the blood-stream in small quantities, hot and moist, is congealed by the action of the fibrine, and this and the unnatural loss of heat cause internal chill and shivering. As the flow of bile increases, its heat overcomes the fibrine and throws it into seething confusion; and if it finally succeeds in getting the upper hand, it penetrates to the marrow, burns through the soul's mooring-cables and sets it free, but if there is less of it and the body resists dissolution, the bile is moistened and expelled from the body either through the pores generally, or, if it is forced through the veins into the upper or lower belly, in the consequent diarrhoea, dysentery and similar disorders, in the course of which it is expelled from the body like an exile in a civil war.

86

44. (d) Note on fevers.

A body that has fallen sick owing to excess of fire produces continuous heat and fever; excess of air causes quotidian fever, of water tertian, water being more sluggish than air and fire. Earth, the most sluggish of the four, needs four times as long to be purged and causes quartan fevers, which are hard to shake off.

45. *Diseases of the soul or mind.*

So much for the way in which diseases of the body occur; we go on to diseases of the soul caused by bodily condition. It will be granted that folly is a mental disease, and of folly there are two kinds, madness and stupidity. Any condition which brings on either must be called a disease; and so we must rank excessive pleasure and pain as among the worst diseases of the mind. For in states of excessive excitement, or of excessive depression caused by pain, a man is in a frenzy of eagerness to grab one thing and avoid another, and at such times is incapable of normal sight or hearing and his reasoning faculty is at its lowest. And when the seed in a man's marrow is full and over-flowing – like a tree producing more than its natural amount of fruit – his desires and their satisfaction cause him on each occasion acute agony and intense pleasure; for most of his life he is maddened by this intensity of pleasure and pain, his soul is deprived of health and judgement by his physical constitution, and he is commonly regarded not as a sick man but as deliberately wicked. But the truth is that sexual incontinence is generally a mental disease caused by a single substance (the marrow) which overflows and floods the body because of the porousness of the bones. And indeed it is generally true that it is unjust to blame over-indulgence in pleasure as if wrongdoing were voluntary; no one wishes to be bad, but a bad man is bad because of some flaw in his physical make-up and failure in his education, neither of which he likes or chooses.

In the same way bodily pains have many bad effects on the mind. Acid and saline phlegm and bitter bilious humours roam about the body, and if they are trapped inside and can get no outlet the vapour that rises from them mixes with 87 the movement of the soul, and the resultant confusion causes a great variety of disorders of different intensity and extent, which attack the three areas where the soul is located with different effects, producing various types of irritability and depression, of rashness and timidity, of forgetfulness and dullness. When, besides all this, men with these flaws of temperament live under bad forms of government where discussion, private and public, is equally bad and where there is no course of study which they can follow from an early age to cure their faults, you have the conditions in which those of us who are wicked acquire our faults owing to two causes entirely independent of our will. The responsibility lies with the parents rather than the offspring, and with those who educate rather than their pupils; but we must all try with all our might by education, by practice and by study to avoid evil and grasp its contrary. That, however, is another story.

46. *The balance of mind and body.*

It is right and proper that we should next look at things from the other side, and explain the treatment by which body and mind are kept healthy; for it is better to devote our attention to good than to evil. The good, of course, is always beautiful, and the beautiful never lacks proportion. A living creature that is to have either quality must therefore be well-proportioned. Proportion in minor matters we perceive and understand easily enough, but we often fail to understand it in matters of major importance. For health and sickness, virtue and vice, the proportion or disproportion between soul and body is far the most important factor; yet we pay no attention to it, and fail to notice that when a strong and powerful mind has too weak and feeble a bodily vehicle, or when the combination is reversed, the whole creature is without beauty, because it lacks the most important kind of proportion. When that proportion is there, on the other hand, you have, for eyes that can see it, the fairest and loveliest of all sights. A body whose legs are too long, or which has some other part disproportionately large, is not only ugly but finds that any coordinated exercise causes it all sorts of trouble, fatigue, strains, and falls owing to its lack of balance. We must expect the same thing in the combination of mind and body which we call a living thing. When the mind is too big for the body its energy shakes the 88 whole frame and fills it with inner disorders; the effort of study and research breaks it down, the stresses and controversies involved in teaching and argument, public or private, rack it with fever, and bring on rheums which deceive most so-called physicians into wrong diagnosis. On the other hand when a large body is joined to a small and feeble mind for which it is too big, of the two natural human appetites, the body's for food and the divinest part's for wisdom, the first is augmented by the influence of the bodily motions which have the upper hand, the second rendered dull, slow to learn and forgetful, and the soul afflicted with the worst of diseases, stupidity. There is one safeguard against both dangers, which is to avoid exercising either body or mind without the other, and thus preserve an equal and healthy balance between them. So anyone engaged on mathematics or any other strenuous intellectual pursuit should also exercise his body and take part in physical training; while the man who devotes his attention to physical fitness should correspondingly take mental exercise and have cultural and intellectual interests. Only so can either rightly be called a fully developed personality.

47. *Physical fitness and the avoidance of drugs.*

The parts of the body should be looked after on the same principles, following the pattern of the universe. For the body is heated and cooled internally by what enters it and dried and moistened by its external environment, and is subject to the disturbances consequent on both processes. If a man yields his body passively to them they overcome it and destroy it; but if he imitates what we have called the nurse and foster-mother of the universe, he will never, if possible, allow his body to remain passively at rest; but will keep it in motion and check the internal and external disturbances to which nature subjects it by compensating movements in himself. By such moderate motion he can reduce to order and system the qualities and constituents that wander through the body according to their affinities, in the same way that we have described in speaking of the universe; and so he will not leave foe ranged by foe to produce conflict and disease in the body, but friend by 89 friend to produce health. Among movements, the best is that we produce in ourselves of ourselves – for it is most nearly akin to the movement of thought and of the universe; next is movement produced in us by another; worst of all is movement caused by outside agents in parts of the body while the body itself remains passive and inert. So the best way of purging and toning up the body is by exercise; next is the motion of a ship or any vehicle that does not cause fatigue; last, and for use in extreme necessity, though not otherwise if we have any sense, is purging by medicine and drugs. Indeed, unless the danger is grave, diseases should not be irritated by drugs. For the course of a disease resembles the life of an animal. Animals are so constituted that there is a set period of life for the species; and for each individual born there is (barring inevitable accidents) an allotted life-span, as its triangles are from the first constituted to last for a certain time, beyond which its life cannot be prolonged. The same is true of the course of diseases; and if their allotted period is interfered with by drugs, they are commonly rendered more serious or more frequent. All kinds of diseases therefore should, so far as leisure permits, be controlled by a proper regime of life, and stubborn complaints should not be irritated by drugs.

48. *Fitness of mind.*

So much then for the living creature as a whole and for its bodily part, and for the way in which a man can train himself and by that training be enabled to lead a rational life. What is far more important is to give the controlling part the training that will best equip it for its work. To deal with this subject in detail would be a considerable task in itself; to us it is a side issue and we shall not be far wrong if we confine ourselves to the following observations, which follow on our previous argument. As we have said more than once, there are housed in us three distinct forms of soul, each having its own motions. Accordingly we may now say, very briefly that any of these forms that lives in idleness and fails to exercise its own proper motions is bound to become very feeble, while any that exercises them will become very strong; hence we must take care that these motions are properly 90 proportioned to each other. We should think of the most authoritative part of our soul as a guardian spirit given by god, living in the summit of the body, which can properly be said to lift us from the earth towards our home in heaven; for we are creatures not of earth but of heaven, where the soul was first born, and our divine part attaches us by the head to heaven, like a plant by its roots, and keeps our body upright. If therefore a man's attention and effort is centred on appetite and ambition, all his thoughts are bound to be mortal, and he can hardly fail, in so far as it is possible, to become entirely mortal, as it is his mortal part that he has increased. But a man who has given his heart to learning and true wisdom and exercised that part of himself is surely bound, if he attains to truth, to have immortal and divine thoughts, and cannot fail to achieve immortality as fully as is permitted to human nature; and because he has always looked after the divine element in himself and kept his guardian spirit in good order he must be happy above all men.[1] There is of course only one way to look after anything and that is to give it its proper food and motions. And the

1. 'Looked after': the word can bear a religious significance in Greek, to 'serve' a god. There is a play on words at the end of the sentence: the word for guardian spirit is 'daemon' and the Greek for happy 'eudaemon'.

motions that are akin to the divine in us are the thoughts and revolutions of the universe. We should each therefore attend to these motions and by learning about the harmonious circuits of the universe repair the damage done at birth to the circuits in our head, and so restore understanding and what is understood to their original likeness to each other. When that is done we shall have achieved the goal set us by the gods, the life that is best for this present time and for all time to come.

49. *The difference between the sexes; creation of women, birds, animals, reptiles and fish.*

I think we may now claim that our original programme – to tell the story of the universe till the creation of man – is pretty well complete. The origin of the other animals can be dealt with quite shortly, and there is no need to say much about it; a brief account on the following lines seems more in keeping with the subject.

The men of the first generation who lived cowardly or immoral lives were, it is reasonable to suppose, reborn in the second generation as women; and it was therefore at that point of time that the gods produced sexual love, constructing in us and in women a living creature itself instinct with life. This is how they did it. What we drink makes its way through the lung into the kidneys and thence to the bladder from which it is expelled by air pressure. From this channel they pierced a hole into the column of marrow which extends from the head down through the neck along the spine and which we have already referred to as 'seed';[1] this marrow, being instinct with life, completed the process and finding an outlet caused there a vital appetite for emission, the desire for sexual reproduction. So a man's genitals are naturally disobedient and self-willed, like a creature that will not listen to reason, and will do anything in their mad

91

1. Cf. p. 101.

lust for possession. Much the same is true of the matrix or womb in women, which is a living creature within them which longs to bear children. And if it is left unfertilized long beyond the normal time, it causes extreme unrest, strays about the body, blocks the channels of the breath and causes in consequence acute distress and disorders of all kinds. This goes on until the woman's longing and the man's desire meet and pick the fruit from the tree, as it were, sowing the ploughland of the womb with seeds as yet unformed and too small to be seen, which take shape and grow big within until they are born into the light of day as a complete living creature.

That is how women and the female sex generally came into being. Birds were produced by a process of transformation, growing feathers instead of hair, from harmless, empty-headed men, who were interested in the heavens but were silly enough to think that visible evidence is all the foundation astronomy needs. Land animals came from men who had no use for philosophy and never considered the nature of the heavens because they had ceased to use the circles in the head and followed the leadership of the parts of the soul in the breast. Because of these practices their fore-limbs and heads were drawn by natural affinity to the earth, and their fore-limbs supported on it, while their skulls were elongated into various shapes as a result of the crushing of their circles through lack of use. And the reason why some have four 92 feet and others many was that the stupider they were the more supports god gave them, to tie them more closely to earth. And the stupidest of the land animals, whose whole bodies lay stretched on the earth, the god turned into reptiles, giving them no feet, because they had no further need for them. But the most unintelligent and ignorant of all turned into the fourth kind of creature that lives in water. Their souls were hopelessly steeped in every kind of error, and so their makers thought them unfit to breathe pure clean air, and made them inhale water, into whose turbid depths they plunged them. That is the origin of fish, snell-fish and everything else that lives in water; they live in the depths as a punishment for the depth of their stupidity. These are the principles on which living creatures change and have always changed into each other, the transformation depending on the loss or gain of understanding or folly.

50. *Conclusion.*

We can now claim that our account of the universe is complete. For our world has now received its full complement of living creatures, mortal and immortal; it is a visible living creature, it contains all creatures that are visible and is itself an image of the intelligible; and it has thus become a visible god, supreme in greatness and excellence, beauty and perfection, a single, uniquely created heaven.

SUMMARY OF CONTENTS OF TIMAEUS
BY NUMBERED SECTIONS

CRITIAS

1. *Introductory Conversation*

TIMAEUS: How glad I am, Socrates, to have brought my 106
story safely to an end, and how pleased to get some rest
after my long journey. I pray the god whose origin we have
just traced in our tale, but who really existed long before,
that we may safely retain all that has been truthfully said, but
pay suitable penalty for any false notes we have involuntarily
struck. And the suitable penalty is that we should correct our
mistakes and play in tune. I pray therefore that god may
grant us knowledge, the most effective and best of all
medicines, so that all we say in future about the origin of
the gods may be true; and with that prayer I hand over to
Critias, as agreed.

CRITIAS: And I am ready, Timaeus. But I must make the
same plea that you made at the beginning, and ask for indulgence because of the magnitude of my theme. Indeed I
think the nature of my subject gives me an even greater 107
claim to it. I know that what I am going to ask will seem
excessive and unnecessarily embarrassing, but ask I must.
No one in his senses could challenge the excellence of the
account you have given: it remains for me to try to show
that my subject is a more difficult one and calls for greater
indulgence. For it is easier, Timaeus, to give a satisfactory
impression when talking to ordinary men about the gods
than when talking among ourselves about mortals. For
inexperience and ignorance of a subject in your audience
make it easy to handle if you are to talk about it; and we
know how ignorant we are about the gods. Let me give you
the following illustration to make my meaning clearer. All
statements we make are inevitably pictures or images. So
let us consider the relative degree of severity with which we
judge the adequacy of the representation by artists of divine
and of human objects. We see that we are satisfied if the

artist can produce quite an elementary likeness of earth,
mountains, rivers and woods, and of the sky and stars and
planets; besides, because of our ignorance of the subject-
matter, we don't subject his pictures to any searching criticism but are content with an imprecise and inaccurate sketch.
But if anyone tries to make a portrait of the human body, we
are, because of our familiarity with it, quick to notice faults
and criticize severely any failure to produce a perfect likeness.
We should recognize that the same is true of verbal descriptions. We are content with faint likenesses when their
subjects are celestial and divine, but we criticize narrowly
when they are mortal and human. So in what immediately
follows, you should make allowances if my narrative is not
always entirely appropriate; for you must understand that it
is far from easy to give satisfactory accounts of human
affairs. It is to remind you of this and to ask for a still greater
108   degree of indulgence for what I am going to say, Socrates,
that I have started with this long introduction. If you think
the favour I'm asking is justified, please grant it.

SOCRATES: Of course we will, Critias; and Hermocrates
may assume that we will grant the same indulgence to him.
For when it is his turn to speak, he will obviously make the
same request as you have; so let him assume the request
granted and proceed without feeling any need of the same
introduction, but rather produce another of his own. But I
warn you, my dear Critias, that the author who preceded
you has made a wonderfully favourable impression on the
minds of his audience,[1] and you will need a lot of allowance
made for you if you are to take over from him.

HERMOCRATES: That warning applies to me as much as
to him, Socrates. But nothing venture nothing have,[2]
Critias; you must tackle your narrative like a man, and call
on Pan and the Muses for their help in singing the praises of
your fellow-citizens of old.

CRITIAS: My dear Hermocrates, you are cheerful enough

1. A reference to the dramatic competition at Athens.
2. The Greek proverb is 'Faint heart never yet set up a trophy'.

because you are still in the rear rank with someone to shelter you. But you will find out soon enough what exposure is like. Meanwhile I must follow your encouraging advice and call on the gods, adding the goddess Memory in particular to those you have mentioned. For my whole narrative depends largely on her. I'm sure my audience will think I have discharged my task with reasonable credit if I can remember adequately and repeat the story which the priests told Solon and he brought home with him. To it I must now proceed without further delay.

2. *Time scale and catastrophe. For the destruction of Athens Atlantis see also* Timaeus, *page 35 ff., and Appendix, p.* 146.

We must first remind ourselves that in all nine thousand years have elapsed since the declaration of war between those who lived outside and all those who lived inside the Pillars of Heracles. This is the war whose course I am to trace. The leadership and conduct of the war were on the one side in the hands of our city, on the other in the hands of the kings of Atlantis. At the time, as we said, Atlantis was an island larger than Libya and Asia put together, though it was subsequently overwhelmed by earthquakes and is the source of the impenetrable mud which prevents the free passage of those who sail out of the straits into the open 109 sea.[1] The course of our narrative as it unfolds will give particulars about the various barbarian and Greek nations of the day; but we must begin with an account of the resources and constitutions of the Athenians and their antagonists in the war, giving precedence to the Athenians.

Once upon a time the gods divided up the Earth between them – not in the course of a quarrel; for it would be quite wrong to think that the gods do not know what is appropriate to them, or that, knowing it, they would want to annex what

1. Cf. *Timaeus*, p. 38, note 1.

properly belongs to others. Each gladly received his just
allocation, and settled his territories; and having done so
they proceeded to look after us, their creatures and children,
as shepherds look after their flocks. They did not use physical
means of control, like shepherds who direct their flock with
blows, but brought their influence to bear on the creature's
most sensitive part, using persuasion as a steersman uses the
helm to direct the mind as they saw fit and so guide the whole
mortal creature. The various gods, then, administered the
various regions which had been allotted to them. But
Hephaestos and Athene, who shared as brother and sister a
common character, and pursued the same ends in their love
of knowledge and skill, were allotted this land of ours as
their joint sphere and as a suitable and natural home for
excellence and wisdom. They produced a native race of
good men and gave them suitable political arrangements.
Their names have been preserved but what they did has
been forgotten because of the destruction of their successors
and the long lapse of time. For as we said before,[1] the survivors of this destruction were an unlettered mountain race
who had just heard the names of the rulers of the land but
knew little of their achievements. They were glad enough to
give their names to their own children, but they knew
nothing of the virtues and institutions of their predecessors,
except for a few hazy reports; for many generations they
and their children were short of bare necessities, and their
minds and thoughts were occupied with providing for
them, to the neglect of earlier history and tradition. For an
interest in the past and historical research come only when
communities have leisure and when men are already provided with the necessities of life. That is how the names but
not the achievements of these early generations come to be
preserved. My evidence is this, that Cecrops, Erectheus,
Erichthonios, Erusichthon and most of the other names
recorded before Theseus, occurred, according to Solon, in
the narrative of the priests about this war; and the same is

1. In the *Timaeus*: see above, p. 35.

true of the women's names. What is more, as men and women
in those days both took part in military exercises, so the
figure and image of the goddess, following this custom, was
in full armour, as a sign that whenever animals are grouped
into male and female it is natural for each sex to be able
to practise its appropriate excellence in the community.

3. *Prehistoric Athens: the land, the people and their institutions.*

In those days most classes of citizen were concerned with
manufacture and agriculture. The military class lived apart,
having been from the beginning separated from the others
by godlike men. They were provided with what was necessary for their maintenance and training, they had no private
property but regarded their possession as common to all,
they did not look to the rest of the citizens for anything
beyond their basic maintenance; in fact they followed in all
things the regime we laid down yesterday when we were
talking about our hypothetical Guardians. And indeed
what we said then about our territory is true and plausible
enough; for in those days its boundaries were drawn at the
Isthmus, and on the mainland side at the Cithaeron and
Parnes ranges coming down to the sea between Oropus on
the right and the Asopus river on the left. And the soil was
more fertile than that of any other country and so could
maintain a large army exempt from the calls of agricultural
labour. As evidence of this fertility we can point to the fact
that the remnant of it still left is a match for any soil in the
world for the variety of its harvests and pasture. And in
those days quantity matched quality. What proof then can 111
we offer that it is fair to call it now a mere remnant of what
it once was? It runs out like a long peninsula from the
mainland into the sea, and the sea basin round it is very deep.
So the result of the many great floods that have taken place
in the last nine thousand years (the time that has elapsed

since then) is that the soil washed away from the high land
in these periodical catastrophes forms no alluvial deposit of
consequence as in other places, but is carried out and lost in
the deeps. You are left (as with little islands) with something
rather like the skeleton of a body wasted by disease; the
rich, soft soil has all run away leaving the land nothing but
skin and bone. But in those days the damage had not taken
place, the hills had high crests, the rocky plain of Phelleus
was covered with rich soil, and the mountains were covered
by thick woods, of which there are some traces today. For
some mountains which today will only support bees produced not so long ago trees which when cut provided roof
beams for huge buildings whose roofs are still standing.[1]
And there were a lot of tall cultivated trees which bore unlimited quantities of fodder for beasts. The soil benefited
from an annual rainfall which did not run to waste off the
bare earth as it does today, but was absorbed in large quantities and stored in retentive layers of clay, so that what was
drunk down by the higher regions flowed downwards into
the valleys and appeared everywhere in a multitude of rivers
and springs. And the shrines which still survive at these
former springs are proof of the truth of our present account
of the country.

This, then, was the general nature of the country, and it
was cultivated with the skill you would expect from a class of
genuine full-time agriculturalists with good natural talents
and high standards, who had an excellent soil, an abundant
water supply and a well-balanced climate. The lay-out of the
city in those days was as follows. The Acropolis was different
112 from what it is now. Today it is quite bare of soil which was
all washed away in one appalling night of flood, by a combination of earthquakes and the third terrible deluge before
that of Deucalion. Before that, in earlier days, it extended to
the Eridanus and Ilisus, it included the Pnyx and was
bounded on the opposite side by the Lycabettos; it was
covered with soil and for the most part level. Outside, on its

1. The reading is uncertain but the sense is fairly clear.

immediate slopes, lived the craftsmen and the agricultural
workers who worked in the neighbourhood. Higher up the
military class lived by itself round the temple of Athena and
Hephaestos, surrounded by a single wall like the garden of a
single house. On the northern side they built their common
dwelling-houses and winter mess-rooms, and everything
else required by their communal life in the way of buildings
and temples. They had no gold or silver, and never used
them for any purpose, but aimed at a balance between ex-
travagance and meanness in the houses they built, in which
they and their descendants grew old and which they handed
on unchanged to succeeding generations who resembled
themselves. In the summer they abandoned their gardens
and gymnasia and mess-rooms and used the southern side
of the Acropolis instead. There was a single spring in the
area of the present Acropolis, which was subsequently
choked by the earthquakes and survives only a few small
trickles in the vicinity; in those days there was an ample
supply of good water both in winter and summer. This was
how they lived; and they acted as Guardians of their own
citizens, and were voluntarily recognized as leaders of the
rest of Greece. They kept the number of those of military
age, men and women, so far as possible, always constant at
about twenty thousand.

This then was the sort of people they were and this the way
in which they administered their own affairs and those of
Greece; their reputation and name stood higher than any
other in Europe or Asia for qualities both of body and
character. I will now go on to reveal to you, as friends,[1] if I
can still remember what I was told when I was a child, the
nature and origin of their antagonists in the war.

1. A reference to a Greek proverb, 'friends share things in
common'.

4. *Atlantis.*
(*a*) *Explanation of nomenclature.*

113   Before I begin, a brief word of explanation, in case you
are surprised at hearing foreigners so often referred to by
Greek names. The reason is this. Solon intended to use the
story in his own poem. And when, on inquiring about the
significance of the names, he learned that the Egyptians had
translated the originals into their own language, he went
through the reverse process, and as he learned the meaning
of a name wrote it down in Greek. My father had his manu-
script, which is now in my possession, and I studied it often
as a child. So if you hear names like those we use here, don't
be surprised; I have given you the reason.

4. (*b*) *Origins: Poseidon and Cleito, their descendants, the natural resources of the island.*

The story is a long one and it begins like this. We have
already mentioned how the gods distributed the whole earth
between them in larger or smaller shares and then established
shrines and sacrifices for themselves. Poseidon's share was
the island of Atlantis and he settled the children borne to him
by a mortal woman in a particular district of it. At the centre
of the island,[1] near the sea, was a plain, said to be the most
beautiful and fertile of all plains, and near the middle of this
plain about fifty stades inland a hill of no great size. Here
there lived one of the original earth-born inhabitants called
Evenor, with his wife Leucippe. They had an only child, a
daughter called Cleito. She was just of marriageable age
when her father and mother died, and Poseidon was attracted
by her and had intercourse with her, and fortified the hill
where she lived by enclosing it with concentric rings of sea
and land. There were two rings of land and three of sea, like
cartwheels, with the island at their centre and equidistant

1. i.e. midway along its greatest length.

136

from each other, making the place inaccessible to man (for there were still no ships or sailing in those days). He equipped the central island with godlike lavishness; he made two springs flow, one of hot and one of cold water, and caused the earth to grow abundant produce of every kind. He begot five pairs of male twins, brought them up, and divided the island of Atlantis into ten parts which he distributed between them. He allotted the elder of the eldest pair of twins his mother's home district and the land surrounding 114 it, the biggest and best allocation, and made him King over the others; the others he made governors, each of a populous and large territory. He gave them all names. The eldest, the King, he gave a name from which the whole island and surrounding ocean took their designation of 'Atlantic', deriving it from Atlas the first King. His twin, to whom was allocated the furthest part of the island towards the Pillars of Heracles and facing the district now called Gadira, was called in Greek Eumelus but in his own language Gadirus, which is presumably the origin of the present name. Of the second pair he called one Ampheres and the other Euaemon. The elder of the third pair was called Mneseus, the younger Autochthon, the elder of the fourth Elasippus, the younger Mestor; the name given to the elder of the fifth pair was Azaes, to the younger Diaprepes. They and their descendants for many generations governed their own territories and many other islands in the ocean and, as has already been said, also controlled the populations this side of the straits as far as Egypt and Tyrrhenia. Atlas had a long and distinguished line of descendants, eldest son succeeding eldest son and maintaining the succession unbroken for many generations; their wealth was greater than that possessed by any previous dynasty of kings or likely to be accumulated by any later, and both in the city and countryside they were provided with everything they could require. Because of the extent of their power they received many imports, but for most of their needs the island itself provided. It had mineral resources from which were mined both solid materials and metals,[1] including one metal which survives today only in name, but was then mined in quantities in a number of localities in the island, orichalc, in those days the most valuable metal except gold. There was a plentiful supply of timber for structural purposes, and every kind of animal domesticated and wild, among them numerous elephants.[2] For there was plenty of grazing for this largest and most voracious of beasts, as well as for all creatures whose habitat is marsh, swamp and river, mountain or plain. Besides all this, the earth bore freely all the aromatic substances it bears today, roots, herbs, bushes and gums exuded by flowers or fruit. There were cultivated crops, cereals which provide our staple diet, and pulse (to use its generic name) which we need in addition to feed us; there were the fruits of trees, hard to store but providing the drink and food and oil which give us pleasure and relaxation and which we serve after supper as a welcome refreshment to the weary when appetite is satisfied – all these were produced by that sacred island, then still beneath the sun, in wonderful quality and profusion.

4. (c) The city and the buildings.[3]

This then was the island's natural endowment, and the inhabitants proceeded to build temples, palaces, harbours and docks, and to organize the country as a whole in the following manner. Their first work was to bridge the rings of water round their mother's original home, so forming a road to and from their palace. This palace they proceeded to build at

1. The contrast is between solid materials like stone and marble and 'fusible' substances, i.e., in the main metals.

2. The first Greek author to mention the elephant is Herodotus in the fifth century (though the Greeks knew ivory long before that). Aristotle has quite a lot about the elephant in his *Historia Animalium*, but this is the only other mention of it before him.

3. See Appendix, p. 152, and Figures 8 and 9.

once in the place where the god and their ancestors had lived, and each successive king added to its beauties, doing his best to surpass his predecessors, until they had made a residence whose size and beauty were astonishing to see. They began by digging a canal three hundred feet wide, a hundred feet deep and fifty stades long from the sea to the outermost ring, thus making it accessible from the sea like a harbour; and they made the entrance to it large enough to admit the largest ships. At the bridges they made channels through the rings of land which separated those of water, large enough to admit the passage of a single trireme, and roofed over to make an underground tunnel; for the rims of the rings were of some height above sea-level. The largest of the rings, to which there was access from the sea, was three stades in breadth and the ring of land within it the same. Of the second pair the ring of water was two stades in breadth, and the ring of land again equal to it, while the ring of water running immediately round the central island was a stade across. The diameter of the island on which the palace was situated was five stades. It and the rings and the bridges (which were a hundred feet broad) were enclosed by a stone 116 wall all round, with towers and gates guarding the bridges on either side where they crossed the water. The stone for them, which was white, black and yellow, they cut out of the central island and the outer and inner rings of land, and in the process excavated pairs of hollow docks with roofs of rock. Some of their buildings were of a single colour, in others they mixed different coloured stone to divert the eye and afford them appropriate pleasure. And they covered the whole circuit of the outermost wall with a veneer of bronze, they fused tin over the inner wall and orichalc gleaming like fire over the wall of the acropolis itself.

The construction of the palace within the acropolis was as follows. In the centre was a shrine sacred to Poseidon and Cleito, surrounded by a golden wall through which entry was forbidden, as it was the place where the family of the ten kings was conceived and begotten; and there year by year seasonal offerings were made from the ten provinces to each one of them. There was a temple of Poseidon himself, a stade in length, three hundred feet wide and proportionate in height, though somewhat outlandish in appearance. The outside of it was covered all over with silver, except for the figures on the pediment which were covered with gold. Inside, the roof was ivory picked out with gold, silver and orichalc, and all the walls, pillars and floor were covered with orichalc. It contained gold statues of the god standing in a chariot drawn by six winged horses, so tall that his head touched the roof, and round him, riding on dolphins, a hundred Nereids (that being the accepted number of them at the time), as well as many other statues dedicated by private persons. Round the temple were statues of the original ten kings and their wives, and many others dedicated by kings and private persons belonging to the city and its dominions. There was an altar of a size and workmanship to match that of the building and a palace equally worthy of the greatness of the empire and the magnificence of its temples. The two springs, cold and hot, provided an unlimited supply of water for appropriate purposes, remarkable for its agreeable quality and excellence; and this they made available by surrounding it with suitable buildings and plantations, leading some of it into basins in the open air and some of it into covered hot baths for winter use. Here separate accommodation was provided for royalty and for commoners, and, again, for women, for horses and for other beasts of burden, appropriately equipped in each case. The outflow they led into the grove of Poseidon, which (because of the goodness of the soil) was full of trees of marvellous beauty and height, and also channelled it to the outer ring-islands by aqueducts at the bridges. On each of these ring-islands they had built many temples for different gods, and many gardens and areas for exercise, some for men and some for horses. On the middle of the larger island in particular there was a special course for horse-racing; its width was a stade and its length that of a complete circuit of the island, which was reserved for it. Round it on both sides were barracks for the main body of the king's bodyguard. A more select body of the more trustworthy were stationed on the smaller island ring nearer the citadel, and the most trustworthy of all had quarters assigned to them in the citadel and were attached to the king's person.

Finally, there were dockyards full of triremes and their equipment, all in good shape.

So much then for the arrangement of the royal residence and its environs. Beyond the three outer harbours there was a wall, beginning at the sea and running right round in a circle, at a uniform distance of fifty stades from the largest ring and harbour and returning on itself at the mouth of the canal to the sea. This wall was densely built up all round with houses and the canal and large harbour were crowded with vast numbers of merchant ships from all quarters, from which rose a constant din of shouting and noise day and night.

4. (d) The rest of the island.

I have given you a pretty complete account of what was told me about the city and its original buildings; I must now try to recall the nature and organization of the rest of the country. To begin with the region as a whole was said to be high above the level of the sea, from which it rose precipitously; the city was surrounded by a uniformly flat plain, which was in turn enclosed by mountains which came right down to the sea. This plain was rectangular in shape, measuring three thousand stades in length and at its midpoint two thousand stades in breadth from the coast. This whole area of the island faced south, and was sheltered from the north winds. The mountains which surrounded it were celebrated as being more numerous, higher and more beautiful than any which exist today; and in them were numerous villages and a wealthy population, as well as

118

141

rivers and lakes and meadows, which provided ample pasture for all kinds of domesticated and wild animals, and a plentiful variety of woodland to supply abundant timber for every kind of manufacture.

Over a long period of time the work of a number of kings had effected certain modifications in the natural features of the plain. It was naturally a long, regular rectangle; and any defects in its shape were corrected by means of a ditch dug round it. The depth and breadth and length of this may sound incredible for an artificial structure when compared with others of a similar kind, but I must give them as I heard them. The depth was a hundred feet, the width a stade, and the length, since it was dug right round the plain, was ten thousand stades.[1] The rivers which flowed down from the mountains emptied into it, and it made a complete circuit of the plain, running round to the city from both directions, and there discharging into the sea.[2] Channels about a hundred feet broad were cut from the ditch's landward limb straight across the plain, at a distance of a hundred stades from each other, till they ran into it on its seaward side. They cut cross channels between them and also to the city, and used the whole complex to float timber down from the mountains and transport seasonal produce by boat. They had two harvests a year, a winter one for which they relied on rainfall and a summer one for which the channels, fed by the rivers, provided irrigation.

4. (e) Military service.

The distribution of man-power was as follows: each allotment of land was under obligation to furnish one leader of a military detachment. Each allotment was ten square stades in size and there were in all 60,000 allotments; there was an unlimited supply of men in the mountains and other

1. Length 3,000, breadth 2,000 (see above): $5,000 \times 2 = 10,000$.
2. Through the canal running through the city: see Figure 9.

parts of the country and they were assigned by district and village to the leaders of the allotments. The leader was bound to provide a sixth part of the equipment of a war chariot, up to a total complement of 10,000, with two horses and riders; and in addition a pair of horses without a chariot, a charioteer to drive them and a combatant with light shield[1] to ride with him, two hoplites, two archers and two slingers, three light-armed stone throwers and three javelin men, and four sailors as part of the complement of twelve hundred ships. Such were the military dispositions of the royal city; those of the other nine varied in detail and it would take too long to describe them.

4. (f) Political and legal authority.

Their arrangements for the distribution of authority and office were the following. Each of the ten kings had absolute power, in his own region and city, over persons and in general over laws, and could punish or execute at will. But the distribution of power between them and their mutual relations were governed by the injunctions of Poseidon, enshrined in the law and engraved by the first kings on an orichalc pillar in the temple of Poseidon in the middle of the island. Here they assembled alternately every fifth and sixth year (thereby showing equal respect to both odd and even numbers), consulted on matters of mutual interest and inquired into and gave judgement on any wrong committed by any of them. And before any prospective judgement they exchanged mutual pledges in the following ceremony. There were in the temple of Poseidon bulls roaming at large. The ten kings, after praying to the god that they might secure a sacrifice that would please him, entered alone and started a hunt for a bull, using clubs and nooses but no

1. In Homeric warfare the charioteer drove the combatant into battle, where he dismounted to fight. (The Greek is obscure. I omit the words $\mu\epsilon$-'$\epsilon\pi\iota\beta\acute{a}\tau\eta\nu$. There is only one combatant and I suspect they were a gloss on $\kappa\alpha\tau\alpha\beta\acute{a}\tau\eta\nu$).

metal weapon; and when they caught him they cut his throat over the top of the pillar so that the blood flowed over the inscription. And on the pillar there was engraved, in addition to the laws, an oath invoking awful curses on those who disobeyed it. When they had finished the ritual 120 of sacrifice and were consecrating the limbs of the bull, they mixed a bowl of wine and dropped in a clot of blood for each of them, before cleansing the pillar and burning the rest of the blood. After this they drew wine from the bowl in golden cups, poured a libation over the fire and swore an oath to give judgement in accordance with the laws written on the pillar, to punish any past offences, never knowingly in future to transgress what was written, and finally neither to give nor obey orders unless they were in accordance with the laws of their father. Each one of them swore this oath on his own behalf and that of his descendants, and after drinking dedicated his cup to the god's temple. There followed an interval for supper and necessary business, and then when darkness fell and the sacrificial fire had died down they all put on the most splendid dark blue ceremonial robes and sat on the ground by the embers of the sacrificial fire, in the dark, all glimmer of fire in the sanctuary being extinguished. And thus they gave and submitted to judgement on any complaints of wrong made against them; and afterwards, when it was light, wrote the terms of the judgement on gold plates which they dedicated together with their robes as a record. And among many other special laws governing the privileges of the kings the most important were that they should never make war on each other, but come to each other's help if any of them were threatened with a dissolution of the power of the royal house in his state; in that case, they should follow the custom of their predecessors and consult mutually about policy for war and other matters, recognizing the suzerainty of the house of Atlas. But the King of that house should have no authority to put any of his fellows to death without the consent of a majority of the ten.

5. Degeneration and punishment.

This was the nature and extent of the power which existed
then in those parts of the world and which god brought to
attack our country. His reason, so the story goes, was this.
For many generations, so long as the divine element in their
nature survived, they obeyed the laws and loved the divine
to which they were akin. They retained a certain greatness of
mind, and treated the vagaries of fortune and one another
with wisdom and forbearance, as they reckoned that qualities
of character were far more important than their present prosperity. So they bore the burden of their wealth and posses- 121
sions lightly, and did not let their high standard of living
intoxicate them or make them lose their self-control, but
saw soberly and clearly that all these things flourish only on
a soil of common goodwill and individual character, and if
pursued too eagerly and overvalued destroy themselves and
morality with them. So long as these principles and their
divine nature remained unimpaired the prosperity which we
have described continued to grow.

But when the divine element in them became weakened
by frequent admixture with mortal stock, and their human
traits became predominant, they ceased to be able to carry
their prosperity with moderation. To the perceptive eye the
depth of their degeneration was clear enough, but to those
whose judgement of true happiness is defective they seemed,
in their pursuit of unbridled ambition and power, to be at
the height of their fame and fortune. And the god of gods,
Zeus, who reigns by law, and whose eye can see such things,
when he perceived the wretched state of this admirable
stock decided to punish them and reduce them to order by
discipline.

He accordingly summoned all the gods to his own most
glorious abode, which stands at the centre of the universe
and looks out over the whole realm of change, and when they
had assembled addressed them as follows: . . .

APPENDIX ON ATLANTIS

It is in the *Timaeus* and *Critias* that the story of Atlantis, whatever its historical origins, first makes its appearance in literature.

At the beginning of the *Timaeus* Socrates recalls a conversation that had taken place the previous day. In it he had described an ideal society with political and social provisions very like those described in the first five books of the *Republic*, but omitting the philosophic and other matters contained in the last five. The conversation referred to cannot be the *Republic* itself, because the *Timaeus* and *Republic* are supposed to take place on festivals that are two months apart: a fairly clear indication by Plato that the *Timaeus* and *Critias* are not to be linked any more closely to the *Republic* then he actually suggests. There is of course some controversy about the relative dates of the three works. The *Republic* is certainly a work of Plato's middle period. The date of the *Timaeus* has been disputed. Let me merely repeat here that I accept the traditional view that it was written in the later period of his life, though precise dating is hazardous. The main point is that the summary we meet in the early part of the *Timaeus* is not an indication of a close connection, but of a deliberate glance back to an earlier work some of the features of which are picked out for purposes of the later dialogue.

After recalling his ideal society in outline Socrates says that he has always been bothered because he can't make it come to life. It is a pretty picture; but would it ever work? It is here that his three companions come in; they are to 'provide a sequel' to what he has described by showing his ideal state in action, 'war' being one of the actions specified.

It is in this context that Atlantis is introduced. Critias proposes to retell an old story, originating with Solon, of a war fought by an earlier Athens against a great power based on an island – Atlantis – in the Atlantic. Socrates' ideal society will be shown existing in this earlier Athens: it will defeat Atlantis, which at the time controlled, within the Straits of Gibraltar, Libya (i.e. Africa) up to the borders of Egypt and Europe as far as Tyrrheria (i.e. Italy): it will restore freedom in the Mediterranean; but will subsequently be destroyed in a great natural cataclysm, which will also swallow up Atlantis. Plato's words are 'Some time later there were earthquakes and floods of extraordinary violence, and in a single dreadful day and night all your [i.e. the Athenian] fighting men were swallowed up by the earth, and the island of Atlantis was similarly swallowed up by the sea and vanished'. And that, incidentally, he adds, is why navigation in the Atlantic is hindered by mud just below the surface, 'the remains of the sunken island'; an extraordinary view which recurs in Aristotle and for which I can give no rational explanation. There is some independent evidence for a belief (possibly based on early Carthaginian voyages) that the Atlantic is shallow, but it remains hard to account for, though it may have suggested the location of Atlantis to Plato.

But that is not all that Critias proposes. Timaeus is to start with an account of the origin of the cosmic system, bringing the story down to man; and as we know from the *Critias*, Hermocrates, the third of the trio, is to finish off, after Critias has told the story of Atlantis, with a further contribution whose subject remains unspecified. I don't think it has been sufficiently noticed what an odd procedure this is. In reply to his comparatively simple question, 'Will my ideal state work?', Socrates has inflicted on him an extremely complex account of the physical world, followed by a piece of imaginary history, followed by an unknown *tertium quid*. And I think it helps to understand Atlantis if we consider this oddity. It has, I suggest, two causes.

1. The Greeks had a bad sense of time. That is what the Egyptian priest in *Timaeus* (to whom we shall return) means when he says, 'you Greeks are all children'; Greek tradition and Greek memory are, he explains, comparatively short. And though the Greeks, both philosophers and others, were interested in origins, they seem to have been curiously lacking in their sense of the time-dimension (there is something about this from a slightly different point of view in Toulmin's *Discovery of Time*). What is more, in so far as they thought of the past they seem to have thought in terms either of degeneration from a perfect primitive state or of cyclic repetition. The idea of degeneration we meet in the *Republic*, Book VII: the idea of cyclic repetition in the *Politicus*. And in the *Timaeus* again we have the notion of periodic destructions by natural cataclysm, followed by a slow re-development of civilization – a notion that recurs once more in Aristotle. Plato is grappling again in *Timaeus*, *Critias* and *Hermocrates* with this problem of development in time, and Atlantis is *part* of one *phase* in it. (Incidentally I very much doubt whether much idea of historical determinism is to be found in him, as Sir Karl Popper suggests. Plato simply didn't think in those terms.)

2. Plato was always plagued by the contrast and conflict of the ideal and the real. With all his greatness he had about him more than a dash of the don and the doctrinaire, of the man who *knows* and the man who will not learn that life simply isn't like that. The *Republic* may have been concerned with principles rather than practice, may not have been intended 'to make a direct contribution to practical politics'.[1] But Plato continued to hope that his principles would have some influence on practice, even though he had seen them founder in Sicily on the rock of human nature that would not tolerate them.[2] And in this trilogy, I suggest, we have yet another attempt to grapple with the problem of the ideal and the real.

1. Crombie, *Examination of Plato's Doctrines* I, p. 76.
2. See my translation of the *Republic* (Penguin second edition 1974), pp. 21–2.

The *Timaeus* gives the religious and philosophical background; the *Critias* a version of earlier history: while the *Hermocrates* was to have brought the story down to the present and grappled with present realities. And perhaps the abandonment of the design had something to do with events in Sicily. There Plato had tried to intervene in the real world, and in Dion had hoped to see a philosopher-king; but in the real and harsh world of Syracusan politics the same Dion became an armed revolutionary. It is difficult to be sure because of dates; the fact that Hermocrates is commonly identified with the fifth century *Syracusan* prominent in the war against Athens is surely not without significance. But may Plato not have felt that he must begin all over again, abandoned his trilogy and turned to the *Laws*, which (as Cornford pointed out) covers much of the ground to be expected in the *Hermocrates*?

Atlantis, then, is part of a middle episode in an attempt to grapple with the problems of human history and the ideal and real in human society. Let us now look at the account in the *Critias* in more detail and then consider some of the questions it raises.

First the alleged origin of the story. Critias says (p. 33) he had it from his grandfather, who in turn had it from Solon, who heard it when he was abroad on his travels in Egypt. To the credibility of this I will return: for the moment I will merely say that it is chronologically possible, if you put the dramatic date of the dialogue at about 425 B.C.

The story is one of a great and successful war waged by antediluvian Athens (Athens before the catastrophe which overwhelmed them both) against Atlantis. There is a brief description of Athens. The land and countryside is more extensive and more fertile than it is in Critias' day, after successive cataclysms have eroded the soil. The institutions are those of the ideal society described by Socrates, with the Guardians (Plato uses the term) living on a rather less bleak and rocky Acropolis. This, with the introductory conversation, brings us more than a third of the way through the fragmentary *Critias*; but in what remains we have had a fairly full description of Atlantis, because when he breaks off in mid-sentence Plato has finished his account of Atlantis, and is about to describe the process of degeneration in the Atlanteans which brings them, as a punishment, into conflict with Athens. He has therefore little more to tell us about Atlantis itself – the rest of the *Critias* would have been concerned with the degeneration of the Atlanteans, the war with Athens and the final catastrophe, about which all we have is the brief summary in the *Timaeus* to which I have already referred.

The account starts with pure myth. When the gods divide up the Earth between them, Atlantis falls to Poseidon. There are already some inhabitants (called earth-born) and (inevitably, one feels) Poseidon falls in love with Cleito, the daughter of two of them. The result is five pairs of twins. They and their naming and the allocation of Atlantis between them take up a rather tedious passage; the only point of importance is that the dynasties they found rule their respective parts of the island absolutely. 'Each of the ten kings had absolute power, in his own region and city, over persons and in general over laws, and could punish or execute at will' (p. 143). And that's about all the politics there was in Atlantis: no question of participation.

When we come to the description of the island we must remember the story of which it is a part. Atlantis is to be a *great* power; the story requires it. Until degeneration it is not a *bad* power – it is, so to say, a hero turned villain, and we are concerned with its heroic phase. And because it is powerful and, initially, approved of, and because it will eventually be defeated and disappear, it will be all to the good if some of its features are strange and unusual. It will have an element of the wonderful about it, or if you prefer the modern term, it will be the first exercise in the art of science fiction. So the temple of Poseidon is a bit outlandish to look at (βαρβαρικόν): so the country's livestock includes elephants, then comparatively unknown, this being their second mention in

Greek literature: so there is a completely unknown and imaginary metal in use, orichalc.

But we must go on with the description. After begetting his twins and enclosing Cleito's original home with rings of water and land (to which we will return) Poseidon fades out, though he remains tutelary god. Atlantis itself is a large island, 'larger than Libya and Asia combined', opposite the Straits of Gibraltar, in the Atlantic. There are other islands in the Atlantic too, and Plato speaks as if the Atlantic were itself enclosed by land which was accessible from these islands. One probably ought not to draw conclusions about Plato's geographical views; but one is reminded of the 'true surface of the earth' in the *Phaedo*, on to which a land-girt, island-studded ocean with the Mediterranean as an offshoot would fit well enough.

To return to the geography of the island. We have seen that it is large, and a good deal of it is mountainous. It has lavish mineral resources (including orichalc), plenty of timber and all kinds of animals (including elephants); and it is generally very fertile. It is longer than it is broad and its longer sides face north and south. In the middle of its south-ern side is an oblong plain 'said to be the most beautiful and fertile of all plains'. This plain is bounded on its seaward side by high cliffs and its natural dimensions are roughly 3,000 stades[1] by 2,000 stades. Irregularities in its rectangular shape have been rectified artificially by a ditch dug round it for purposes of irrigation in the form of a rectangle of 3,000 by 2,000 stades. This ditch or canal is a stade wide. Cross ditches are dug at intervals of 100 stades from the landward to the seaward limb of the ditch; and channels also connect these cross ditches. Plato is a bit vague about these channels; he says that 'the whole complex was used to float down timber from the mountains and to transport seasonal produce'. And it is tempting to envisage the whole system as a vast chequer board. But Plato is not definite and makes a mistake in his mathematics, failing to allow for the width

1. A stade is very slightly less than a furlong.

of the cross ditches in his calculations. Yet the pattern must surely have been symmetrical, and the chequer board is the easiest assumption. The only other thing worth noting here is that the mountains surrounding the plain are said to be large and beautiful, with a large and wealthy population and abundance of timber and other natural resources.

But what Plato is most interested in and spends most time describing is the capital city itself, and more particularly its inner citadel. At the central point of the citadel is the original home of Cleito and Poseidon. This is a low hill about 50 stades inland. An outer wall, circular and with a radius of about 50 stades, surrounds it. And the city is therefore thought of as a circle, lying between the seaward irrigation canal and the coast and touching both tangentially. Its outer wall is densely built up with houses but that is all we hear about it.

This part of Plato's description is shown in Figure 8. It assumes a chequer-board pattern for the canals; and notice that the irrigation system has its outlet to the sea through a canal that runs through the city. The inner citadel is shown as a series of small rings at the centre, and it is that inner citadel that Figure 9 illustrates. Its basic form was determined by Poseidon who ringed the small hill where Cleito lived with two rings of land and three of water; but its equipment and buildings are the work of the inhabitants.

Details are as follows:
The breadth of the rings of land and water is $3+3$, $2+2$, and 1 stade, and the central island is 5 stades across. (Is it significant that this gives a total of $27 = 3^3$?) Each land ring is surrounded by a wall; ring 1 is plated with orichalc, ring 2 with tin, ring 3 with bronze. The water rings are *bridged*, and the land rings *pierced* by roofed underpasses for triremes. These are shown as rather awkwardly coinciding at their ends: which does not so much matter for the underpasses, but *is* awkward for the final bridge whose outer end must coincide with the inner end of the *canal to the sea*, which leads out of it and to which corresponds a *canal leading to the*

irrigation system. To finish off these features of general lay-out the bridges have *guard-houses* at their ends (7: it is not clear whether at both ends or one) and we are told that each ring and the central island is appropriately garrisoned. Stone for building is quarried from rings and island and pairs of underground docks constructed in the process (10).

The *central island* contains

6 The royal palace.

4 Shrine of Poseidon and Cleito plus temple of Poseidon, 'rather outlandish', and surrounded by a golden wall.

5 Baths, supplied by hot and cold springs (separate accommodation for royalty, commoners, women and horses), and the grove of Poseidon.

The ring-islands have temples, gardens, gymnasia and barracks; and the outer, larger island has a horse-racing stadium running all round it.

One should perhaps add in conclusion:

1. That there is a military organization that is a sort of cross between Sparta and Homer: Sparta, in that the land is distributed in allotments ($\kappa\lambda\hat{\eta}\rho o\iota$ 119a) which carry an obligation to military service; Homer, in that chariots are still the major weapon of war.

2. That control is in the hands of the ruling dynasty (descendants of the twins) who have as we have seen absolute power, and who meet periodically for consultation which takes place with a lot of ritual, a lot of dressing up, and the catching of a bull followed by its ritual sacrifice.

What are we to make of all this?

We must remember Plato's purpose – to describe a rich, powerful and technologically advanced society to serve as an opponent of his ideal Athens. He had a fertile imagination and in Atlantis produced (I have suggested) the first work of science fiction. And (using that description in its widest sense) his Atlantis has been widely influential; he certainly started something. But we must be very careful about reading meanings into his narrative. Some things are clear enough. Hippodamus had already planned cities, and

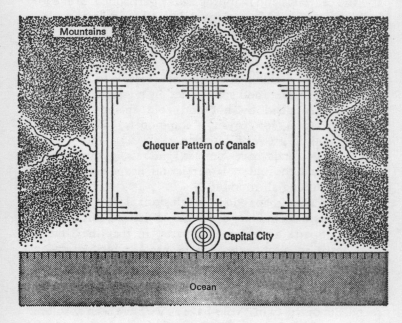

FIGURE 8

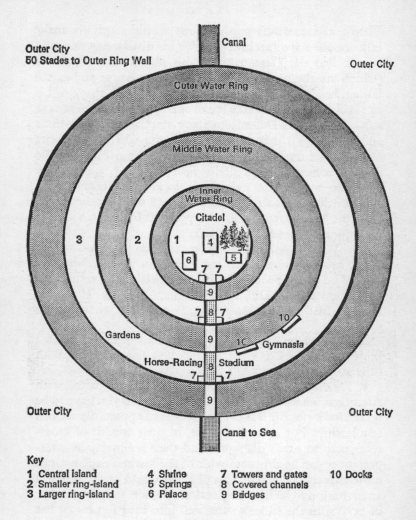

Figure 9 — diagram labels:

Canal

Outer City
50 Stades to Outer Ring Wall

Outer City

Outer Water Ring

Middle Water Ring

Inner Water Ring

Citadel

Outer City

Gardens

Horse-Racing Stadium

Gymnasia

Outer City

Canal to Sea

Key
1 Central island   4 Shrine   7 Towers and gates   10 Docks
2 Smaller ring-island 5 Springs   8 Covered channels
3 Larger ring-island   6 Palace   9 Bridges

FIGURE 9

Plato's mathematical predilections would naturally make him choose a symmetrical plan for his canals. Anyone who has studied the *Timaeus* knows his obsession with circles (which are the governing force in the universe and in the human head) and cannot be surprised that the shape of his city is circular – no need to look for Babylonian influences as some have done. Indeed once you start on interpretations and influences it is hard to stop. Perhaps Cleito's five pairs of twins are due to the importance of the decad. But the decad is commonly regarded as the sum of 1, 2, 3, 4: so why did Plato not give her a singleton, twins, triplets and quadruplets? Such speculations are profitless, whether they come from the learned, with elaborate parallels from Plato's other dialogues, or merely from cranks.

But Plato's Atlantis, besides starting a new literary form, has of course been the source of endless speculation. And that speculation has centred largely round the simple question. 'Did Plato invent Atlantis?' If he did then no further question arises. If not then what was his source?

Replies can be grouped into three categories, of which I must discuss the first two very quickly. They are dealt with fully in James Bramwell's *Lost Atlantis*.

1. *The crazy*. There is no doubt that a preoccupation with Atlantis often leads to a certain craziness, and you have to be on the look-out for this even in works of apparently serious scholarship. For learned articles, in their wealth of cross-references to other dialogues and their ingenuity of interpretation, can be almost as wide of the mark as explanations more naïvely crazy. The idea of a lost world or continent is an invitation to let the imagination run riot, and the number of books on the subject runs well into four figures (it has been estimated at 5,000). The first and perhaps the best known of the more recent in the series is Ignatius Donelly's *Antediluvian World*, published in America in 1882. It supposes there to have been, as Plato said there was, a lost continent where the Atlantic now is, and to it and to its

inhabitants attributes the origin of almost everything. Luce's summary is not unfair:

'There was once a land connection between Europe and America; ergo Atlantis. Primitive and cultured people all the world over have Deluge legends; ergo Atlantis. Peruvian and Mexican civilizations were as advanced as anything in the old world; ergo Atlantis. Having accepted all this one is in no mood to question such propositions as "Genesis contains a history of Atlantis" or "The Carians of Homer are the same as the Caribs of the West Indies".'[1]

And Bramwell tells us that the theosophists and occultists have had their say about Atlantis as well. Nor need you, if you don't like it, stick to the location in the Atlantic; the hunt for alternative sites is all part of the game.

But none of this, bar the initial suggestion of a lost continent, has much to do with Plato.

2. The second type of reply can be called the *geological*. This attempts to keep within the bounds of fact by producing scientific evidence for the existence of an Atlantic continent at some earlier phase in the earth's history. There is a raised ridge in the Atlantic, running from Iceland to the South Atlantic, and surfacing at the Azores, Ascension Island and Tristan da Cunha; and some geologists have held that it is the remains of a landbridge between Europe and America. There are, in addition, quite a number of legends on the Atlantic seaboard about lands and cities engulfed by the ocean, which, it can be argued, indicate a thread of human memory going back to a great inundation. And there are of course problems of human origins, cultural parallels and distribution of flora and fauna which can be fitted neatly into a lost Atlantis, as Lewis Spence has done in his books on the subject.

But the geologists are not agreed: the time scales don't fit easily; legends of lost cities can be accounted for by known and comparatively minor shifts of coastline and sea level; and when Lewis Spence argues that the suicidal habits of the

1. *The End of Atlantis*, p. 42.

Norwegian lemming are due to a migratory habit directing it to lost Atlantis, fact has surely again been swallowed up in fantasy.

In any event all this again has little to do with Plato, or with his Egyptian priests, whose memory may have been long but whose records hardly stretched back into geological time. The latest summary of this particular argument by Galanopoulos and Bacon (who are quite capable of their own flights of fancy) runs as follows: 'There never was an Atlantic landbridge since the arrival of man in the world: there is no sunken land mass in the Atlantic: the Atlantic ocean must have existed in its present form for at least a million years. In fact it is a geophysical impossibility for an Atlantis of Plato's dimensions to have existed in the Atlantic'.[1] And this judgement seems to be a fair statement of present geophysical opinion.

3. So we come to the third type of answer, the *historical*. First, how serious is Plato in his story about Solon and the Egyptian priests? Taylor, who spent a lifetime trying to prove that every word Plato wrote was historically based, rather surprisingly says that we could hardly be told more plainly than we are by Plato's narrative that the whole story is a fiction. And yet it is precisely in this sort of detail – date, setting, relative ages, personalities – that Plato is often at his most realistic. The sequence Solon/Dropides – Critias/grandfather – Critias/grandson is chronologically possible. And I am prepared to go so far as to say that there may be *some* foundation in fact in Plato's tale. But what foundation? Again I would maintain that we cannot expect much detail and will probably mislead ourselves if we look for it. But Solon might have heard a story of a powerful island people overwhelmed by some natural disaster; and perhaps of its involvement at one point in an unsuccessful war, though I should be very hesitant about this, for Plato's ideal antediluvian Athens is clearly a deliberate fiction. The only other expectation which seems reasonable is that the story

1. *Lost Atlantis*, p. 75.

should have been of a purely Mediterranean disaster in historic time.

The historical answer to which I now come was first suggested by K. T. Frost in 1913, in an article in the *Journal of Hellenic Studies* whose title indicates its thesis – 'The *Critias* and Minoan Crete'. Frost's thesis in short is that in the Atlantis story we have a reminiscence of Minoan Crete. Assuming the Solon story to be true, at least in essentials, he asks, in effect, to what powerful island civilization and its destruction could the Egyptian records have referred? We know that there certainly was contact between Egypt and Minoan Crete, and Frost rehearses the evidence. And if *our* few extant Egyptian records have references to Crete may there not have been more in Solon's day? Atlantis is of course not in the Mediterranean. But, to an Egyptian, Crete was north-westerly, and the west was traditionally the place of fable and mystery, of the golden apples and the gates of Hades, and of Homer's Phaeacians, also sometimes regarded as a Minoan reminiscence; and these two factors are enough to account for the displacement. Again, we must beware of details. I don't really believe that the Atlantic mud is the quicksands of Syrtes; nor do Frost's other details convince. There may indeed be a Minoan cup showing a bull caught in a net; but I can see no real connection between Plato's rather complex ritual and what we know of the bull of Minos.

But one key piece of evidence was not available to Frost. The great island in the west must be overwhelmed in a natural disaster; and we have today a suitably-dated disaster to fill the bill. In 1939 Professor Marinatos drew attention to the volcanic explosion which overwhelmed the island of Santorini, or to use its ancient name, Thera, in the fifteenth century B.C. and suggested that it might be responsible for the widespread destruction which took place in Crete at the end of the century, after which the island never recovered its former prosperity.

First, a distinction. There are two questions to be answered: 'Could Minoan Crete have been overwhelmed by earthquake and volcanic explosion?' and 'Could any inkling of this have reached Plato?'

It is with the first of the two questions that I begin.

I have used the phrase 'volcanic explosion' because the eruption of Thera was no ordinary eruption like for example that which overwhelmed Pompeii. What it was like we know from the explosion of Krakatoa in the East Indies in 1883 (there have been similar explosions, one for example at Tambora in the same area; but Krakatoa is the best documented). In this sort of volcanic action it is not a matter of the mere flow of lava and ash. There is an underground accumulation of volcanic matter (magma) followed by an explosion which blows a great hole in the earth. The results are pretty startling. The explosion of Krakatoa was heard in Western Australia, three thousand miles away: most of Krakatoa disappeared: clouds of volcanic ash turned day to night as far as 160 miles away, and caused particularly fine sunsets all over the world that year; there was a great tidal wave and at distances up to eighty kilometres away waves averaged fifteen metres high, while a small warship at anchor in harbour ended up two miles inland. It should be added that both Thera and Krakatoa lie on major fault lines, and that the 1883 explosion was preceded by 'six or seven years of earthquakes'.[1]

You will notice that there are three main features in the process. The fall of ash, the tidal wave, and the associated earthquake which need not be precisely contemporaneous. That there was an explosion of this kind at Thera is unquestionable, and doubted by no one. Its antecedents and effects are more difficult to assess in detail. In Thera its destruction was absolute. A great deal of it simply disappeared. On what remains there is clear evidence of Minoan settlement, and excavations, started under the late Professor Marinatos, are still in progress. And the wider effects of the

1. Luce, op. cit., p. 76.

explosion have similarly to be assessed on a combination of seismological and archaeological evidence.

The earliest published investigation of Thera was by Fouqué, *Santorini et ses éruptions* (Paris 1879). He was concerned with the seismological and geological evidence; he did some excavation, but he wrote before Evans's excavations in Crete and what he has to say reads rather quaintly today. The most complete recent treatment from the seismological point of view is by two Americans, Ninkovich and Heezen (Colston Papers, 1965).

The date of the explosion seems to have been some time in the fifteenth century. Carbon 14 dating is never very precise, but the consensus of tests that have been made points to such a date; and it has long been accepted by archaeologists that there was a general destruction of Minoan sites sometime in the latter part of the century. There is growing agreement that the two events – the explosion and the destruction – are connected; and both types of evidence point to the second half of the fifteenth century, though it is worth adding that the final explosion of Thera may have been preceded by a series of earlier eruptions and earthquakes of less intensity. (And here we may clear up a minor point. Plato talks of the destruction of Atlantis as having taken place nine thousand years before his day. But he had little idea of time and dating, as we have seen, and it is just possible that a misunderstanding of the original figures could have led to multiplication by ten; which would bring one back to about the date which we have just established.) But when we come to consider the extent of the final disaster, we learn that the caldera (or crater caused by the explosion) is four times larger at Thera than at Krakatoa. Simple multiplication is no doubt not permissible, but the figure gives some idea of the scale of the disaster. Let us look at the three features I have enumerated.

First, the ash. Ninkovich and Heezen are able to quote the evidence of cores taken from the sea-bed, which show a widespread fall of volcanic ash, drifting on the heat storm produced by the combination of the explosion and the prevailing northwest wind, and so not affecting the mainland or much of the Aegean. But the fall in central and east Crete would have been considerable. If one takes Ninkovich and Heezen's figures for cores taken from the sea, it seems likely that there was an average fall of 20 cm, and probably in many places rather more. Such a fall would destroy all vegetation and make the affected area uninhabitable for a period up to a generation. Estimates of the tidal wave which must have occurred vary widely (from 50 to 600 feet): nor is it easy to be sure of its path. And the particular kind of destruction which archaeology has found seems unlikely to be due to flooding. It may be that the deep water between Thera and Crete would absorb the shock; tidal waves run highest in narrow and shallow waters. On this factor therefore I can feel no certainty: there must have been a tidal wave, but its effects may have been restricted, though it is likely to have wrecked harbours and ships.

When we come to the third factor, the earthquake, we can again speak with more certainty. We have seen that it is generally accepted by archaeologists that there was widespread destruction in central and east Crete in the latter part of the fifteenth century. The type of destruction, the collapse of buildings followed by fire, is that caused by earthquake damage, and it seems reasonable to suppose that it was so caused, and that the explosion of Thera was associated with a major earthquake. The joint result was a devastation from which Minoan civilization never recovered. There was material and cultural decline and political domination by Mycenae.

That this was the general picture seems reasonably certain. It is more difficult to reconstruct events in detail but it may be that what happened was somewhat as follows. In the first quarter of the fifteenth century there was an eruption on Thera which destroyed the Minoan settlement there (archaeological evidence shows that the destruction took place before the final disaster in Crete). At about the same time there seems to have been some earthquake damage at Cnossos, necessitating considerable repairs though no major reconstruction. The subsequent period at Cnossos was that of the so-called Palace style of pottery, showing Mycenaean influence, and of the Linear B Tablets, which, being in Greek, again show Mycenaean influence, indeed perhaps domination, for a change of language is likely to indicate a change of political control. Perhaps the earthquake damage at Cnossos, even if not major, gave the Mycenaeans the chance to extend their influence. The course of events in the middle and later part of the century is uncertain, and archaeologists are not agreed. But it seems easiest to suppose that the final destruction affected all sites alike, rather than that Cnossos alone in a measure survived (in archaeological terms, to follow those who suppose that periods Late Minoan I B & II are contemporaneous). The latest dateable archaeological find from this period (an Egyptian seal at Hagia Triada) is dateable to the late fifteenth or early fourteenth century, and the commonly accepted date for the final disaster about 1400 B.C. Thereafter, as we have seen, the story is one of cultural decline and Mycenaean domination. Idomeneus at Troy is subordinate to Agamemnon.

The answer, therefore, to my first question, 'Was Minoan Crete overwhelmed by a natural catastrophe?' is Yes. I turn to my second question, 'Could Plato have had any inkling of this?' If we accept the Solon story as possible at all, then I think it is equally possible that it may have contained a reference to a powerful and highly civilized island in the west overwhelmed by earthquake and flood. The Egyptians were in touch with Crete and would be likely to hear something of the Thera catastrophe; and if Krakatoa is anything to go by they would have had some direct experience of its effects. (Australia is further from Krakatoa than Egypt from Thera). Nor does it seem to me in the least surprising that the story should occur only in Plato. By his own account it had survived as, so to speak, a bit of family gossip in Critias' family. There was nothing in the Greek mind or memory to connect it with Crete, and all Plato did (if he did anything) was to pick it up as something he could incorporate in his latest account of early human history. The details are all his own (there were no elephants in Crete), and any hunt for correspondence of detail between Atlantis and Minoan Crete is a wild goose chase. It is tempting, as one stands on the site of Phaestos, looking over the plain of Messara, to suppose that this is the low hill on which the citadel of Atlantis was built, that Phaestos was Atlantis and the plain of Messara (with suitable irrigation works) the 'most beautiful of all plains' described by Plato. But it is a temptation to be resisted. For Plato's purpose was not in any proper sense historical. He was concerned yet again with a conflict which plagued him (as in different forms it plagues us all) throughout his life. At its deepest, most philosophical level it is the conflict between appearance and reality, between fleeting experience and eternal truth; at its political level it is the conflict between principle and practice, between what we think ought to be and what regrettably is. He had dealt with this conflict in the *Republic* where we find the philosophical background, the principles on which society ought to be organized, and then in Books VII and VIII the regrettable degeneration into the world of politics we know. How far the historical form in which in the *Republic* Plato casts this degeneration is to be taken seriously, is a matter for argument. But he returns to the idea again in the *Timaeus, Critias, Hermocrates* trilogy. The *Timaeus* deals again with the problem of change and permanence, and brings it closer to the real world because it is concerned, for most of its length, with physical reality. The *Critias* deals, professedly, with an early period of human history, though it is history with a strong element of myth in it, witness the appearance of Poseidon and Cleito. Could the ideal ever have been realized? Yes, says Plato; and it would have defeated any opposition however powerful. Not (I think) a very convincing way of making Socrates' lay figures come to life. But it is what Plato did. In the *Hermocrates* he would surely have had to come to closer grips with the world of political reality, as he had in the *Timæus* with the world of physical reality. Why did he break off with the job only half-finished? If Hermocrates the Syracusan had any association in his mind with Dion, perhaps sadness at seeing a potential philosopher-king engulfed in the harsh realities of political life made him reluctant to continue. More likely, he felt that the design of the trilogy was unsatisfactory, that the central problem of transferring political ideals to real life needed different treatment – treatment he attempted in the *Laws*. Atlantis was a by-product in the whole process, but one that has been to later generations an inspiration of doctrinal fancy and of fictional other worlds.

But if Atlantis was a by-product, one incident in a much wider canvas, nonetheless it is not without its modern revelance. I have suggested that the *Critias* is the first essay in science fiction. For science fiction there seem to be two motives. First, the attempt to peer into the future and guess what man's growing control over nature may enable him to do. This motive, you will say, can hardly have operated with Plato. Yet if Atlantis is situated in the past, it is nonetheless a society with an advanced material civilization, a construction by the imagination of what man's ingenuity could achieve. There is a certain similarity. The other motive is, to put it unkindly, the wish to escape from reality. Most of us, if we are honest, know that much of what we read is read to relax the mind, to take it away from its preoccupations in a weary life and let it escape into another realm. We each have our particular choice. You may find your anodyne in sentimental romance or in a detective story. Some science fiction adds sentiment to speculation, as in the story in which the hero first sees the heroine in a bubble-bath on board a space ship. Plato was not given to that particular kind of escapism. But in the story of Athens and Atlantis he had yielded to escapism of another kind. For surely if you cannot see how your Utopia can ever work in the real world, it is mere escapism to project it either into the distant past or into the distant future. But many others have followed him down this particular escape route.

When men think about politics they tend to think either about the world as it is or about the world as they would wish it to be. The tension between these two opposite ways of thinking is probably needed if we are to retain any balance. But each of them has its dangers. If you look at life as it is you may well feel how fragile a thing political order is, something built up over the years with much care and sacrifice. You will become legitimist, traditionalist, conservative, prepared for change only on good pragmatic grounds. Yet society needs its critics, men cannot live without faith, without the burning desire to right what they see as wrong. But in the real world good intentions alone are not enough; they harden easily into dogma and intolerance. Plato's *intentions* were admirable; and he could give a shrewdly realistic analysis that can fit painfully well in places today: if you want an account of the permissive society turn to the *Republic*, Book VIII – 'the teacher fears and panders to his pupils ... their elders try to avoid the reputation of being disagreeable or strict by aping the young and mixing with them on terms of easy good fellowship'. Yet in the *Republic* he sketched a society that is surely by any human standards intolerable, and the gap between it and the needs and possibilities of the human beings who must live and suffer in the real world is aptly symbolized by the rather desperate attempt in the *Critias* to pretend that it *could* exist and indeed *had* existed, but far away and long ago. This kind of pretence does no one any good; on the contrary it is the source of much human suffering, because it tempts us to sacrifice people to principles. Examples in our own time are ready enough to hand. I will content myself with a brief concluding reference to Milovan Djilas's book, *The Unperfect Society*. The word *un*perfect is used deliberately to contrast with what Djilas calls 'the perfect, or classless society', which is the goal, as I would say the illusory goal, of so many well-intentioned people today.

And here is Djilas's own explanation, a fit comment on all Utopians from Plato onwards:[1]

I need perhaps to explain here my use of the word 'unperfect', with which I seek to make a semantic distinction from the more common 'imperfect'. As the chapters that follow will illustrate, it is my belief that society cannot be perfect. Men must hold both ideas and ideals, but they should not regard these as being wholly realizable. We need to comprehend the nature of utopianism. Utopianism, once it achieves power, becomes dogmatic, and it can quite readily create human suffering in the name and in the cause of its own scientism and idealism. To speak of society as imperfect may seem to imply that it can be perfect, which in truth it cannot. The task for contemporary man is to accept the reality that society is unperfect, but also to understand that humanist humanitarian dreams and visions are necessary in order to reform society, in order to improve and advance it.

1. Milovan Djilas, *The Unperfect Society*, p. 2.

BIBLIOGRAPHY

THE various theories about Atlantis that have been put forward since Plato are reviewed in James Bramwell's *Lost Atlantis* (Cobden-Sanderson, 1937). Some of the more far-fetched suggestions that have been made will be found in Ignatius Donelly's *Atlantis: the Antediluvian World* (New York: revised edition, 1949); and an example of the geological type of speculation is Lewis Spence's *The Problem of Atlantis* (London, 1924). K. T. Frost's identification of Atlantis as Minoan Crete was made in an article in the *Journal of Hellenic Studies*, Vol. 33, 1913. An up-to-date version of this view can be found in J. V. Luce, *The End of Atlantis* (Thames & Hudson, 1969), which contains references to the main sources for the seismological evidence, of which the most detailed is Ninkovich and Heezen's *Santorini Tephra* (Colston Papers, 1965). A very readable attempt, based on Plato's description of the destruction of Atlantis, to account for the end of the Minoan–Mycenaean civilization in terms of seismology, climatic change and archaeology is Professor Rhys Carpenter's *Discontinuity in Greek History* (Cambridge University Press, 1965). Finally there are Professor Denys Page's Northcliffe lectures, published by the Society for the Promotion of Hellenic Studies (Supplementary Paper No. 13, 1970) under the title *The Santorini Volcano and the Desolation of Minoan Crete*. Professor Page was kind enough to discuss some of his conclusions with me while these lectures were still in the press.

Discover more about our forthcoming books through Penguin's FREE newspaper...

Penguin Quarterly

It's packed with:

- exciting features
- author interviews
- previews & reviews
- books from your favourite films & TV series
- exclusive competitions & much, much more...

Write off for your free copy today to:
Dept JC
Penguin Books Ltd
FREEPCST
West Drayton
Middlesex
UB7 0BR
NO STAMP REQUIRED

READ MORE IN PENGUIN

In every corner of the world, on every subject under the sun, Penguin represents quality and variety – the very best in publishing today.

For complete information about books available from Penguin – including Puffins, Penguin Classics and Arkana – and how to order them, write to us at the appropriate address below. Please note that for copyright reasons the selection of books varies from country to country.

In the United Kingdom: Please write to *Dept. JC, Penguin Books Ltd, FREEPOST, West Drayton, Middlesex UB7 0BR*

If you have any difficulty in obtaining a title, please send your order with the correct money, plus ten per cent for postage and packaging, to *PO Box No. 11, West Drayton, Middlesex UB7 0BR*

In the United States: Please write to *Penguin USA Inc. 375 Hudson Street, New York, NY 10014*

In Canada: Please write to *Penguin Books Canada Ltd 10 Alcorn Avenue, Suite 300, Toronto, Ontario M4V 3B2*

In Australia: Please write to *Penguin Books Australia Ltd, 487 Maroondah Highway, Ringwood, Victoria 3134*

In New Zealand: Please write to *Penguin Books (NZ) Ltd, 182–190 Wairau Road, Private Bag, Takapuna, Auckland 9*

In India: Please write to *Penguin Books India Pvt Ltd, 706 Eros Apartments, 56 Nehru Place, New Delhi 110 019*

In the Netherlands: Please write to *Penguin Books Netherlands B.V., Keizersgracht 231 NL–1016 DV Amsterdam*

In Germany: Please write to *Penguin Books Deutschland GmbH, Friedrichstrasse 10–12 W–6000 Frankfurt/Main 1*

In Spain: Please write to *Penguin Books S. A., C. San Bernardo 117–6° E–28015 Madrid*

In Italy: Please write to *Penguin Italia s.r.l., Via Felice Casati 20, I–20124 Milano*

In France: Please write to *Penguin France S. A., 17 rue Lejeune, F–31000 Toulouse*

In Japan: Please write to *Penguin Books Japan, Ishiki-ibashi Building, 2–5–4, Suido, Bunkyo-ku, Tokyo 112*

In Greece: Please write to *Penguin Hellas Ltd, Dimocritou 3, GR–106 71 Athens*

In South Africa: Please write to *Longman Penguin Southern Africa (Pty) Ltd, Private Bag X08, Bertsham 2013*

READ MORE IN PENGUIN

READ MORE IN PENGUIN

A CHOICE OF CLASSICS

Hesiod/Theognis	**Theogony and Works and Days/ Elegies**
Hippocrates	**Hippocratic Writings**
Homer	**The Iliad**
	The Odyssey
Horace	**Complete Odes and Epodes**
Horace/Persius	**Satires and Epistles**
Juvenal	**Sixteen Satires**
Livy	**The Early History of Rome**
	Rome and Italy
	Rome and the Mediterranean
	The War with Hannibal
Lucretius	**On the Nature of the Universe**
Marcus Aurelius	**Meditations**
Martial	**Epigrams**
Ovid	**The Erotic Poems**
	Heroides
	Metamorphoses
Pausanias	**Guide to Greece (in two volumes)**
Petronius/Seneca	**The Satyricon/The Apocolocyntosis**
Pindar	**The Odes**
Plato	**Early Socratic Dialogues**
	Gorgias
	The Last Days of Socrates (Euthyphro/ The Apology/Crito/Phaedo)
	The Laws
	Phaedrus and Letters VII and VIII
	Philebus
	Protagoras and Meno
	The Republic
	The Symposium
	Theaetetus
	Timaeus and Critias

READ MORE IN PENGUIN

A CHOICE OF CLASSICS

Plautus	**The Pot of Gold/The Prisoners/The Brothers Menaechmus/The Swaggering Soldier/Pseudolus**
	The Rope/Amphitryo/The Ghost/A Three-Dollar Day
Pliny	**The Letters of the Younger Pliny**
Pliny the Elder	**Natural History**
Plotinus	**The Enneads**
Plutarch	**The Age of Alexander** (Nine Greek Lives)
	The Fall of the Roman Republic (Six Lives)
	The Makers of Rome (Nine Lives)
	The Rise and Fall of Athens (Nine Greek Lives)
	Plutarch on Sparta
Polybius	**The Rise of the Roman Empire**
Procopius	**The Secret History**
Propertius	**The Poems**
Quintus Curtius Rufus	**The History of Alexander**
Sallust	**The Jugurthine War** and **The Conspiracy of Cataline**
Seneca	**Four Tragedies** and **Octavia**
	Letters from a Stoic
Sophocles	**Electra/Women of Trachis/Philoctetes/Ajax**
	The Theban Plays
Suetonius	**The Twelve Caesars**
Tacitus	**The Agricola** and **The Germania**
	The Annals of Imperial Rome
	The Histories
Terence	**The Comedies (The Girl from Andros/The Self-Tormentor/TheEunuch/Phormio/The Mother-in-Law/The Brothers)**
Thucydides	**The History of the Peloponnesian War**
Virgil	**The Aeneid**
	The Eclogues
	The Georgics
Xenophon	**Conversations of Socrates**
	A History of My Times
	The Persian Expedition